▲◤● | English 3D™
HMH

ISSUES

COURSE A • VOLUME 1

Printed in the U.S.A.

ISBN 978-0-358-60949-0

r7.23

6 2024

4500884376

TABLE OF **CONTENTS**

Debate

How much screen time is too much?

Look around. Do you see a glowing screen? It's likely! Smartphones are everywhere. So are televisions, video game systems, tablets, and computers. Screens connect us to people. They entertain us. They also help us learn new information. Screens make our lives easier and more fun.

But do we spend too much time in front of screens? It turns out that too much screen time can mess up how we sleep at night. Screens can also make it harder to pay attention. And even though using screens helps us multitask, are they stopping us from a job well done?

How much screen time is too much? Let's dig deeper and find out!

New technology has kids more plugged in than ever. Is it time to step away from screens?

Virtual Reality ·····························

Almost **99%** of children report watching television each day.

(Source: The National Center for Health Statistics, 2014)

Screening Screen Time ···············

Doctors recommend limiting screen time to less than **2 hours** each day.

66% of children and teenagers say their parents have "no rules" about time limits and media.

(Source: American Academy of Pediatrics, 2013)

Double Digital ·····························

Children spend an average of **7.5 hours** in front of screens each day. That's more time in front of screens than in school!

A study found that children spend **26%** of their screen time using two **digital devices** at the same time.

(Source: The Henry J. Kaiser Family Foundation, 2010)

R U 2 Plugged In?

by Joe Bubar from *Scholastic News*

Ten-year-old Megan Rivera is never too far from a screen. On a normal day, she spends hours after school texting with friends. She puts photos on Instagram. She does her homework while watching her favorite TV shows. The fifth grader says she can't imagine her life without screens.

"I would be bored all the time," Megan says.

Many other kids spend much of their free time using **devices** with screens. They play games, watch videos, or send texts. Today's kids are connected to technology like no generation before.

That has many adults worried. They fear that screens may be taking over kids' lives. Scientists say spending too much time in front of screens can be bad for your health.

Some experts think kids who spend too much time using screens can become **addicted** to them.

> **Today's kids are connected to technology like no generation before.**

Screen Overload

Computers, TVs, video game systems, smartphones. In today's world, it's nearly impossible to avoid screens. That's not necessarily a bad thing. In many ways, screens make our lives easier. Phones and computers connect us with friends. They help us do research for school projects. In fact, some health experts say relaxing by watching TV or playing games is fine in small amounts.

The problem is that many kids spend more time on these **devices** than they should. Doctors recommend that kids limit their screen time to less than two hours a day. But on average, American kids spend about seven and a half hours a day with screens. According to doctors, all that extra screen time could **lead to** problems. These problems range from weight gain to trouble sleeping. Too much screen time can also **lead to** lower grades in school.

Digital Distractions

Being surrounded by screens can make it hard to **focus** on one task. In a recent study, researchers in California observed students doing their homework. After just two minutes, many kids

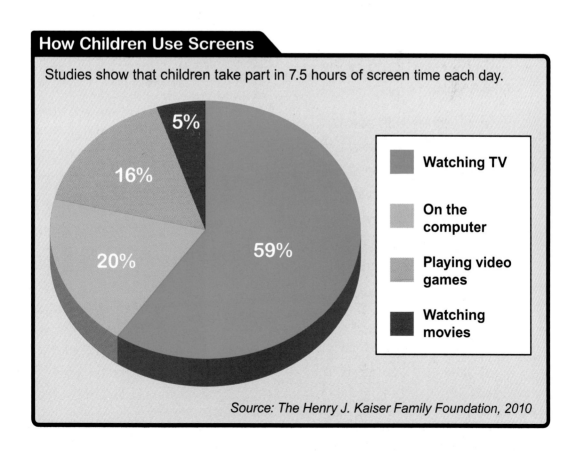

How Children Use Screens

Studies show that children take part in 7.5 hours of screen time each day.

5%

16%

20%

59%

- Watching TV
- On the computer
- Playing video games
- Watching movies

Source: The Henry J. Kaiser Family Foundation, 2010

started surfing the Internet. Some kids were texting. They had stopped **focusing** on their work. Experts say that using a lot of **digital devices** allows you to do many things at once, but none of them well.

"Switching between tasks takes up brainpower," says Dr. Victoria Dunckley. Dr. Dunckley is a psychiatrist. She helps many young people who struggle with too much screen time. "So not only does it take you longer to get the task done, but you do the task with less accuracy," she says.

Spending too much time in front of screens can be bad for your health.

Screens can also cause kids to have trouble shutting down at night. Studies have shown

Experts say using digital devices is fine in small amounts.

that using **digital devices** right before bedtime can keep you tossing and turning all night.

"Even small amounts of technology use after sundown tricks the brain into thinking it's daytime and impacts sleep," Dr. Dunckley explains.

She adds that it's important to take plenty of screen breaks during the day, too. This helps "to allow the brain to rest." Dr. Dunckley suggests that kids use that extra time to **communicate** face-to-face with one another instead.

Technology CONTENT CONNECTION

Digital Citizenship

Being a good digital citizen means that you act responsibly and appropriately when using technology. Just like citizens in the real world, digital citizens follow rules for how to behave online. They also are careful about the information they post or share. As a digital citizen, it's important to remember: if you wouldn't do or say something to someone in person, you shouldn't do it online either.

Here are some tips to be a better digital citizen:

- Always treat others the way you want to be treated, online or offline.
- Only communicate with people you know.
- Read and reread emails and messages before pressing "send."
- Think twice about posting pictures and personal information.

TAKE A STAND

Should there be rules for how we act online?

Debate

DOES RECESS GIVE YOUR BRAIN A BOOST?

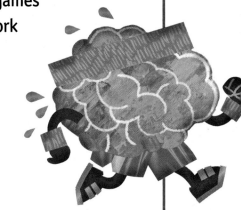

Is recess just about having fun? Maybe not! Studies show that having recess can help you focus and learn better once you're back in the classroom.

But experts argue that what you do during recess matters. Some think students should have organized games with rules. Coaches teach students how to work together. Other experts think students need a break from rules during recess. They think students should have time for free play, like running around or climbing a jungle gym.

Let's stretch our minds—and bodies—and learn more about recess!

Recess is an important part of the school day for students' brains and bodies. Are you getting enough?

Down With Bullying ···················

A study found that there was **43%** less bullying in schools with a **structured** recess program.

(Source: Mathematica Policy Research, 2013)

Principals Agree ······················

In a survey of almost **2,000** principals, researchers found that:

- **66%** of principals report that students listen and focus better after recess.

- **96%** of principals believe that recess helps students' **social development**.

(Source: Robert Wood Johnson Foundation, 2010)

Let's Move—More! ·····················

Only **5** states say that schools must have daily recess for elementary school students.

The Centers for Disease Control and Prevention (CDC) suggests that students in elementary school should have **20 minutes** of recess a day.

(Source: Centers for Disease Control and Prevention, 2014)

The Power of Play

Experts study play, and learn it's more than fun and games.

by Jennifer Marino Walters from *SuperScience*

Jared Bardar, a fifth grader from Wadsworth, Ohio, sprints after his friends trying to make them "it." Almost every day, he plays tag, swings on the monkey bars, or runs around the neighborhood. What do these activities have in common with eating vegetables and doing homework? More than you think!

Secret Brain Booster

Experts say children need play to help **develop** their minds and bodies. A recent study of 11,000 third graders **found** that kids who get more than 15 minutes of recess daily concentrate and behave better than those who get little or no recess.

But the same study **found** that 30 percent of kids don't get any recess, or get too little of it. That's because schools across the United States have been cutting back on recess to increase class time. The thinking is that more time for lessons helps raise students' test scores and grades.

"PLAY IS DISAPPEARING FROM THE LIVES OF CHILDREN."

"Play is disappearing from the lives of children," says Joan Hoffman. She's a play expert at Strong National Museum of Play in Rochester, New York.

Power Play

Play comes in many different forms. Many kids get lots of **structured** play. **Structured** play includes activities like tennis lessons and organized sports. When kids play tag, stage a made-up play, or run around a playground, they are **participating** in **unstructured** play, or free play.

"Free play is voluntary, it's fun, and it's done for its own sake," says Dr. Stuart Brown. He's the founder of the National Institute for Play. Free play is the type of play that experts say kids need most.

Free play helps kids **develop** strong and healthy bodies. It also helps them avoid obesity, and build confidence. "Playing helps me when I'm stressed," says Jared. "It makes me feel happy and energetic."

Free play also helps kids **develop** many **social** skills they will need as adults. For example, free play can help kids with problem solving and working together. It can also help with reading facial expressions. "Many things kids will need in their jobs, they can learn through play," says Hoffman.

Finally, play is a way for kids to take a much-needed break. "Recess gives me a chance to not think about

Students who get more than 15 minutes of recess every day concentrate and behave better.

schoolwork for a while," says Olivia Vigna. Olivia is a sixth-grader from West Point, New York.

Play Every Day

Kids who don't have daily recess can still get many of the benefits of play on their own time. Hoffman says kids should aim for at least 20 minutes of free play daily.

That can include anything from climbing on a jungle gym at the park to playing hide-and-seek with friends.

But chances are that kids don't need an adult to tell them to play. "The desire to play comes from deep within us," says Dr. Brown. "It's a natural part of being alive."

Have you gotten your daily dose of play today?

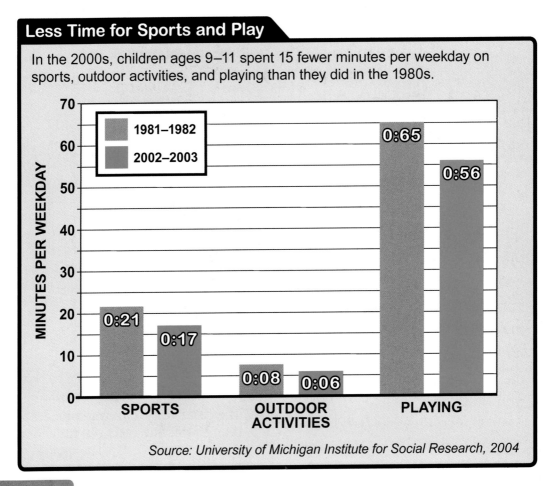

Less Time for Sports and Play

In the 2000s, children ages 9–11 spent 15 fewer minutes per weekday on sports, outdoor activities, and playing than they did in the 1980s.

Legend: 1981–1982, 2002–2003

MINUTES PER WEEKDAY

SPORTS: 0:21, 0:17
OUTDOOR ACTIVITIES: 0:08, 0:06
PLAYING: 0:65, 0:56

Source: University of Michigan Institute for Social Research, 2004

To Fix the Classroom, Rethink Recess

by Lois Kazakoff from the *San Francisco Chronicle*

1 After years of hand-wringing about our public schools, educators are **finding** improved work in the classroom— by encouraging play.

"Good recess is essential for good learning," said Wendy Forrest. She's the principal of Montalvin Elementary School in San Pablo, California. There, lessons from the playground have **transformed** the school.

Teachers **found** that after 20 minutes of energetic **structured** play, students return to their desks refreshed. They settle down quickly, so more time is spent on teaching. As a result, test scores at Montalvin are rising. Suspensions and referrals are down. There was but one fight in the whole of the last school year. This is a big difference from just two years ago, Forrest said.

Better yet, students who were always late have started showing up early so they would have a chance to play with a friend, noted Montalvin sixth-grade teacher Shelley Moore. Kids stopped hanging

The rules for jump rope are simple: take turns, and look out for others.

out in cliques where they spent recess gossiping and bickering. In short, the school has become a place where kids want to be.

TEACH KIDS HOW TO PLAY? WHAT HAS HAPPENED TO RECESS?

❷ Until two years ago, though, "What was happening in the schoolyard was taking away from classroom instruction," Forrest said. That was before the school partnered with Playworks. Playworks is a nonprofit organization started 17 years ago in Oakland, California. It is now in 22 US cities after catching the attention of the Robert Wood Johnson Foundation.

Playworks' program is simple: it brings full-time coaches to schools to teach kids how to play.

Teach kids how to play? What has happened to recess?

When I was a child, recess was where the action was. But that was then.

Now parents in many neighborhoods fear street violence, so they keep their children indoors. "Play" involves a computer screen, not a kickball. Left on a schoolyard for recess, students don't know what to do.

Yet the day I visited Montalvin, Playworks' "Coach Pete" Best had nearly every student in organized games or activities. When the primary grades spilled out onto the upper playground, games of tether ball, wall ball, kickball and four square started right up. A group gathered at the basketball hoop to play H-O-R-S-E. Three kids began whirling hula hoops. Third-graders waited in line to spike a volleyball back to a purple-shirted sixth-grade girl serving as a junior coach.

On the lower field, the upper grade students also quickly **structured** games. No child is

required to **participate**, but very few sat through recess. There was a small group of girls chatting about stuffed animals they had lined up on a cement wall. One third-grader was finishing a worksheet.

Coach Pete, 30, has spent more than a decade working with children. But he credits Playworks with turning him into an effective teacher. While he draws from a playbook of 362 games, his lessons are not about the rules.

"The secret sauce is play itself," said Playworks founder Jill Vialet. "Play is an opportunity to model the skills of empathy, teamwork, leadership, and inclusion."

To understand Playworks' **effect**, Forrest had the students write about recess. One boy wrote: "I could talk to Coach Pete about how I was feeling."

Another child wrote: "I became the winner for once."

Health CONTENT CONNECTION

Making Healthy Decisions

Every day, we make choices that affect our health. Many of the decisions are about food. Should I eat an apple or a candy bar? Extra bread or extra salad? These little decisions can add up to big health benefits.

Similarly, we can make healthy choices about our physical activity. The US Department of Health and Human Services recommends that children do 60 minutes of physical activity every day. So when you have the option to go for a bike ride instead of playing video games, or walk home instead of taking the bus, make a healthy decision. The minutes can really add up!

TAKE A STAND

What healthy choices can you make to increase your daily physical activity?

Debate

Should we bring extinct animals back to life?

Every year, thousands of types of animals disappear from the earth. The cause of their disappearance is simple and well known. It's us.

When humans cut down forests or pollute rivers and oceans, they have an effect on the animals that live there. We take away animals' homes and we change what food is around for them to eat. Sometimes, animals can't adjust. They die out, or become extinct.

Some scientists are trying to bring back animals that have died out. They argue it's the right thing to do. Not everyone agrees.

Should scientists bring back extinct animals? Or should humans work harder to protect animals and their homes before they disappear?

As the human population grows, our need for space and natural resources like wood and oil does too. What does that mean for animals?

Animal Populations Down

The numbers of mammals, birds, fish, amphibians, and reptiles in the world have decreased by **52%** in the past **40 years**.

(Source: World Wildlife Fund, 2014)

Endangered Species

There are over **1,000** **species** of animals that are listed as **endangered** worldwide.

(Source: US Fish & Wildlife Service, 2014)

Congress passed the Endangered Species Act (ESA) in **1973**. This means the government has the responsibility to protect **endangered** or threatened animals and the places that they live.

(Source: National Wildlife Federation, 2014)

Disappearing Homes

Every minute, an area of forest the size of **36** football fields is cut down.

Researchers predict that **60%** of the world's coral reefs, which are home to many plant and animal species, will be gone by **2033**.

(Source: World Wildlife Fund, 2013)

They're Back!

Long-extinct species are not quite back, but scientists may soon be able to re-create the creatures. Should they?

by Bryan Walsh from *TIME for Kids*

❶ Each year, an estimated 10,000 to 100,000 animal **species** die off. They join the countless **species** that have gone **extinct** over the course of Earth's history—and **extinction** means forever.

At least it used to. Scientists are now closing in on the **ability** to bring back **extinct**

The body of this baby mammoth was found after being frozen in a riverbank for 40,000 years. Scientists studied her body and collected her DNA to learn more about her life.

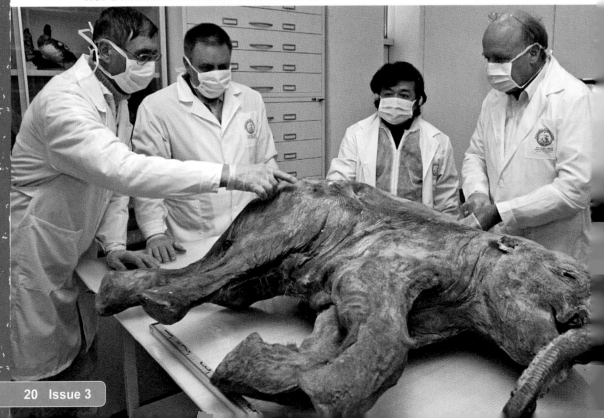

ability to bring back **extinct species**. No, this doesn't mean the plot of *Jurassic Park* is going to become a reality. Researchers need DNA to bring back a **species**. DNA is the chemical that carries the structure for a living thing. Dinosaurs have been gone too long for any of their DNA to remain in fossils.

But there's a very real chance that we will be able to bring back more recently extinguished **species**. This could even include Ice Age animals like the woolly mammoth. In 2003, a team of Spanish and French scientists re-created the Pyrenean ibex, which had gone **extinct** three years earlier. The new animal didn't **survive** long, but scientific advances should improve the success rate. In January 2013, Australian scientists announced that they were on their way to

Endangered Species in the United States

There are 281 vertebrate species that are listed as endangered in the United States. A vertebrate is any animal that has a spine or backbone.

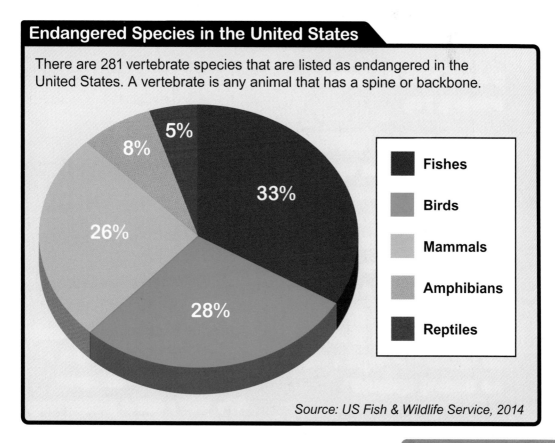

■	Fishes
■	Birds
■	Mammals
■	Amphibians
■	Reptiles

Source: US Fish & Wildlife Service, 2014

The Pyrenean ibex (left) and gastric brooding frog (below) are two species that scientists are working on bringing back from extinction.

bringing back the gastric brooding frog.

❷ Correcting Mistakes

Just because we can bring a **species** back doesn't mean that we should. There may be **benefits** to reviving a **species**. But there's no way to know how it will turn out. For example, would a passenger pigeon fit into its old habitat? Or might it crowd out existing **species**?

Scientists are now closing in on the ability to bring back extinct species.

Environmentalists worry that our **ability** to bring **species** back might cut down support for the hard work of traditional conservation. Why worry about **preserving** a wildlife habitat or fighting poachers if we know we can just **reverse** our mistakes?

But those **extinctions** are our mistakes to correct, which may give us an obligation to do so. As businessman and environmentalist Stewart Brand recently said, "Humans have made a huge hole in nature. We have the **ability** now . . . to repair some of that damage."

We would do well to remember the lesson of *Jurassic Park*: proceed with caution. And maybe leave the velociraptors be.

Science   CONTENT CONNECTION

What is an ecosystem?

An ecosystem is a community of living things like bacteria, plants, and animals, and the environment that they live in. For example, a forest is an ecosystem with living plants and animals like trees, shrubs, bears, owls, and squirrels, and nonliving things like soil, rocks, sunlight, and water. The plants and animals in an ecosystem depend on one another and the nonliving things to survive. If one part of the ecosystem is taken away, it has an effect on all the other elements of the ecosystem.

TAKE A STAND

What would happen if one plant or animal species in an ecosystem went extinct?

Buffalo Dusk

by Carl Sandburg from _Smoke and Steel_

The buffaloes are gone.

And those who saw the buffaloes are gone.

Those who saw the buffaloes by thousands and how they

pawed the prairie sod into dust with their hoofs,

their great heads down pawing on in a great pageant

of dusk,

Those who saw the buffaloes are gone,

And the buffaloes are gone.

Bringing Back the Buffalo

When this poem was written in 1922, the American bison, also known as the buffalo, was nearly **extinct**. The population had shrunk from tens of millions to less than a thousand. The animals were often hunted for their skins, which could be sold for a lot of  money. Then, some ranchers captured and began to breed a few of the animals. Today, American bison herds are found roaming throughout the West. The National Bison Association estimates that there are around 340,000 buffalo in North America today.

Meet the Author

CARL SANDBURG

Born: January 6, 1878, in Galesburg, Illinois

Died: July 22, 1967, in Flat Rock, North Carolina

Articles, Poems, and Books: Sandburg started his writing career as a journalist. He wrote news articles for the *Chicago Daily News.* In his career as an author, Sandburg wrote poetry, novels, biographies, and children's books. His most well-known works include: *Cornhuskers, Rootabaga Stories,* and *Abraham Lincoln.*

Prize-Winning Author: Carl Sandburg won three Pulitzer Prizes, two for his poetry and one for his biography of Abraham Lincoln. He also won a Grammy Award in 1959, in the category of *Best Performance– Documentary or Spoken Word.*

Debate Is it time to dump bottled water?

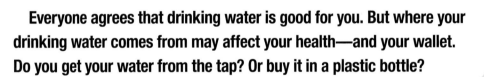

Everyone agrees that drinking water is good for you. But where your drinking water comes from may affect your health—and your wallet. Do you get your water from the tap? Or buy it in a plastic bottle?

For many, tap water is free and easy to get at home. But it can be hard to find on the go. For others, tap water is unsafe to drink, so bottled water is the only option. The problem is that plastic bottles create pollution. Each year, billions of plastic bottles litter our land and oceans. And plastic bottles can take up to 100 years to disintegrate.

Does the harm of plastic bottles outweigh the benefits? Should we get rid of plastic bottles?

Bottled water is an easy way to stay hydrated, but the bottles create a lot of garbage. Is a quick drink worth the endless plastic trash?

Plastic Planet

The United States creates around **32 million tons** of plastic waste each year.

(Source: Environmental Protection Agency, 2014)

The Power of Plastic

The amount of energy saved by **recycling 1** plastic bottle is enough to light a 60-watt light bulb for **6** hours.

Americans buy over **29 billion** bottles of water each year.

(Source: National Geographic, 2011)

Recycle, Reduce, Reuse

In the United States, about **30%** of the plastic bottles that were used were **recycled**.

Up to **2,785 million pounds** of plastic bottles are collected for **recycling** each year.

(Source: American Chemistry Council, 2012)

The Bottled Water Debate

from *Storyworks*

Last year, Americans bought 31 billion bottles of water. Stack those bottles up, and the plastic tower would stretch from Earth to the moon and back eight times!

Why do we love bottled water so much? It's **convenient**. Just grab a bottle and go. Then toss it out when you're done. It's healthy too, compared with sugary sodas and drinks. And it's much better than tap water.

Or is it?

In fact, one-fourth of all bottled water is tap water. Many top-selling brands sell tap water that has been run through a **filter**.

It turns out that waters bottled from springs and streams aren't necessarily better than the water you can get from your kitchen sink. In taste tests, tap water often wins. And chances are that the water flowing from your tap has been tested more than what you find in a bottle. That's because most cities regularly test tap water. They want to make sure it doesn't contain dangerous germs or chemicals. Bottled-water companies don't have to test as rigorously.

33 million bottles a day wind up in landfills.

But the main criticism of bottled water isn't the quality of the water—or even the fact that Americans are paying for water they can get for free. It's those plastic bottles. Though they can be **recycled**, few actually are. Seventy-two percent of plastic bottles are thrown into the trash. Actually, 33 million bottles a day wind up in landfills, where they will sit for hundreds of years.

One billion people do not have access to safe water.

These mountains of trashed plastic bottles have inspired a growing number of communities to take action. The town of Concord, Massachusetts, **banned** the purchase of bottled water. And some college campuses are doing the same. At Cherry Tree Elementary School in Indiana, kids get reusable water cups with their lunch. Bottled water is still for sale, but most kids simply raise their hands at lunch and hold up three fingers. That's Cherry Tree's sign for "I want water, please." The program has been a big success.

But not everyone can simply choose to avoid

Drinking bottled water helps people stay hydrated.

bottled water. Around the world, one billion people do not have access to safe water. If they drank from the tap or from local supplies, they could get seriously sick or even die. For them, bottled water isn't a **convenience**. It's life or death.

In addition, **banning** bottled water could lead people to drink more unhealthy beverages, like soda. And these sugary drinks contribute to America's growing problem with obesity.

Still, it seems that America might be losing its thirst for bottled water. Sales are slowing down. Sales of reusable water bottles are soaring. And many towns want to **ban** the sale of bottled water.

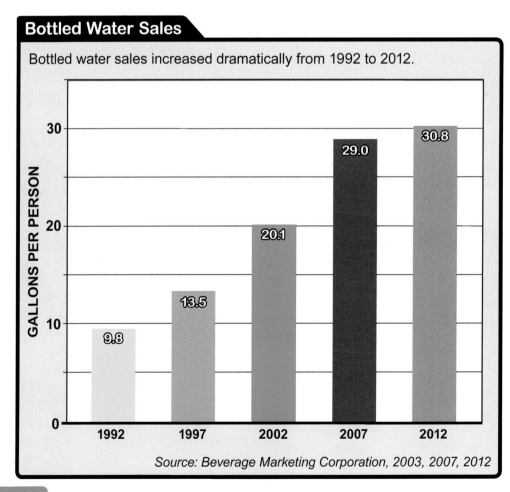

Bottled Water Sales

Bottled water sales increased dramatically from 1992 to 2012.

GALLONS PER PERSON

Year	Gallons
1992	9.8
1997	13.5
2002	20.1
2007	29.0
2012	30.8

Source: Beverage Marketing Corporation, 2003, 2007, 2012

Think About What You Drink

Drinking water is one of the healthiest things you can do for your body. There's no argument about that. But what to drink?

by Lynn Brunelle from *Current Health Teens*

❶ Hydration Nation

Your body is made up of about 65 percent water. Every day you lose water through sweating, breathing, and urinating. So every day you need to replace that fluid to keep your body running smoothly. A lot of the water you need comes from the foods you eat. Fruits and vegetables are mostly water. But you should also drink water for good health.

So how much do you need? There are many factors to consider, such as your age, weight, and activity level. "An average 110-pound kid needs about two liters of fluid a day," according to Dr. Maureen

Reusable water bottles are one solution to single-use plastic water bottles.

Koval, a family practitioner in Bainbridge Island, Washington. "But that's all fluid, from all beverages and whatever food you eat." Drink to satisfy your thirst and even more if you are exercising or if it's really hot outside.

Big Business

Bottled water is big business—about $100 billion annually. The bottled water industry has created a huge market by banking on the need for portable drinking water and promoting the idea of fresher, cleaner water. At a markup of as much as one

Tap water can be up to one thousand times cheaper than bottled water.

thousand times the cost of tap water, there is much money to be made.

Bottled Up

Is bottled water better than tap? Not all companies **regulate** the water that goes into their bottles. A study conducted in 1999 by the Natural Resources Defense Council, an **environmental** group, found that "an estimated 25 percent or more of bottled water is really just tap water in a bottle."

Clearly, that's not what many bottled water buyers think they're getting. "If it says 'natural spring water' on the label, it probably comes from a groundwater source. But these days up to 40 percent of bottled water is simply repackaged tap water," says John Stewart, national organizer of the *Think Outside the Bottle* campaign.

Annoyed about that practice? You're not alone. "Bottled water tastes good and it's **convenient**, but the idea of companies packaging tap water and selling it back to me just bugs me," says Kate S., 17, of Colorado.

Stewart's group wants the practice of repackaging tap water to change. "We're working to get major bottlers of water to state clearly on their labels where their water comes from," he says. And those efforts are making a difference. Grassroots actions such as petitions, call-in days, and letter-writing campaigns have put pressure on large bottled water companies. The response has been good. Soon many labels will be clear about where the water actually comes from.

❷ Is Plastic so Fantastic?

A lot of oil and energy go into every bottle of water. Huge amounts of energy are used to produce the bottles and package the water. Those bottles are shipped hundreds of miles from the bottling companies to the stores. And transporting them

burns even more oil.

Safety **concerns** also exist. The chemicals used to make the bottles are safe. However, toxins can leak into the water if the bottles are exposed to extreme heat or cold. Recent studies show that chemicals called phthalates, which may disrupt hormones, can seep into the water from the plastic bottle. Not much is known yet about the potential health risks, but you may be getting more than you bargained for when you

Up to 40% of bottled water is simply repackaged tap water.

drink from a plastic bottle.

What happens to the plastic after you drink the water? The good news is that plastic is **recyclable**. The bad news is that not all bottles are **recycled**. Around 30 percent of plastic water bottles get **recycled**. "More than four billion pounds of plastic end up in landfills and along the roadside every year," says Stewart.

The Big Drip

The federal Food and Drug Administration (FDA) sets standards for bottled water. The Environmental Protection Agency (EPA) sets standards for public water supplies. But their rules aren't the same. As a result, there can be a big difference in how bottled water and tap water compare in terms of safety.

"Tap water comes from reservoirs and is tested for contaminants hundreds of times a month," says Stewart. "Public water systems also have annual reports **available** so you can check on the health of your local tap water. Less than one percent of the FDA's time and resources is spent on **regulating** bottled water. So many of the companies are left to police themselves."

Chemical Additives

Does your tap water taste funny? Public water can have small amounts of good or not-so-good chemicals that can change the taste. Chlorine is added in many public water systems to kill germs, but it can leave an aftertaste. Another chemical, fluoride, may be added to public water because it is helpful in preventing tooth decay.

Not all chemicals are intentionally put in, though. Pipes can shed lead or rust. In certain parts of the country, runoff from nearby farms can taint the water.

A good **filter** can help. Tabletop pitchers with charcoal **filters** can absorb and remove chemicals and leave the tap water tasting fresh. Other **filters** placed directly on the tap can remove chemicals and small particles before they pass through the faucet.

Tapping In

So the next time you're thirsty, drink up. But think about what you drink. "We're not saying bottled water shouldn't exist," says Stewart. "In emergency situations it's great. But clean drinking water is a human right and a public good, one you shouldn't have to pay so much for."

If only bottled water is **available**, drinking it is OK.

Staying healthy is important. But if you have a choice, reaching for a glass or finding a fountain may make a big difference for the planet.

Just ask Isaac G., 14, of Washington. He says: "I drink both tap and bottled water, but I choose tap water whenever I can. It just makes more sense for me—and for the **environment**."

Social Studies CONTENT CONNECTION

Zero Waste

Imagine a world without growing landfills. San Francisco, California, is trying to make that dream a reality. The city has a goal of Zero Waste by the year 2020. What's Zero Waste? Zero Waste means preventing trash from becoming . . . well . . . trash. Instead, garbage is reused in clean and helpful ways. Citizens are required to separate their trash into recyclable, compostable, and landfill trash cans. The recyclable trash, like plastic, is reused. The compostable trash, like old food, is turned into nutritious soil for local farmers. And although landfill-bound trash is still present, it has been reduced significantly. Through new legislation and responsible citizens, San Francisco is leading the way to a cleaner California.

TAKE A STAND

Should all cities aim for San Francisco's goal of Zero Waste by 2020?

Debate

Should We Plug In to Wind and Solar Energy?

Refrigerators. Televisions. Cell phones. They all need power to work. But where does power come from?

Most power comes from factories. They are called power plants. The plants burn oil, coal, or gas to create power. Then the power travels through wires or pipes to your home.

But burning oil, gas, and coal causes pollution. Some people think power from the wind or sunlight is a better idea. It is clean power that doesn't pollute. But the price is high. Wind and solar plants also take up a lot of space.

Should we switch to wind and solar power? Let's learn more!

Data File

When it comes to energy, how important is using renewable power from the wind and sun?

Old-School Fuel ·····················

About **65%** of dangerous greenhouse gases, like carbon dioxide, come from burning fossil fuels like coal, oil, and natural gas.

(Source: Ecofys, 2013)

Power Play ·······························

In 2013, fossil fuels like coal and natural gas produced **66%** of America's electricity. Renewable resources like wind and sun **generated 13%**.

In 2012, US wind power **generated** enough **energy** to provide electricity to more than **12 million** homes.

(Source: US Energy Information Administration, 2014)

Turnoffs ·····························

Some studies say that up to **440,000** birds are killed by wind turbines each year.

(Source: Energy Informative, 2014)

Solar power plants are expensive to build. Large plants like Ivanpah can cost over **$2.5 billion** to create.

(Source: The Washington Post, 2014)

Mighty Wind

A huge offshore wind farm opens off the British coast. Is the United States next?

from *Scholastic News*

Winds of change are blowing overseas. In late September 2010, the world's largest wind farm opened off the southeast coast of England. The farm has 100 giant windmills called wind turbines. Its builders say it can produce enough electricity to power 200,000 homes.

Wind turbines work like a fan in reverse. Wind spins the turbines' giant blades. That motion powers a **generator**, which creates electricity that runs through underwater cables to get to land.

Offshore wind farms use underwater cables to send electricity to land.

Most electricity comes from burning coal and natural gas, which creates pollution. Wind is a cleaner **renewable energy** source. Unlike coal and other fossil **fuels**, wind will never run out.

But not everyone is a fan of wind farms. Some critics say they cost too much to build and are unreliable because wind speed often changes. Others simply don't like looking at the big turbines.

Some people in the US have been making these arguments against offshore wind farms. The US is the world's top wind-power producer. Soon it will have its own offshore wind farm. A 130-turbine wind farm called Cape Wind is planned off the coast of Massachusetts. After years of debate, the US government finally approved the project in October 2010. Construction is set to start in 2015.

How Wind Turbines Work

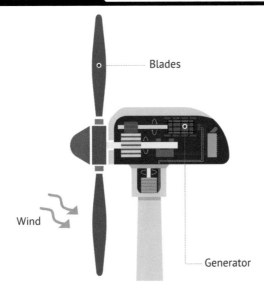

Blades

Wind

Generator

❶ Wind blows over the blades of a wind turbine, causing them to rotate.
❷ Inside the wind turbine, a shaft turns with the blades. This shaft is connected to a generator.
❸ The generator creates electricity as all of the pieces turn.

Bright Future

by Cody Crane from *Science World*

Deep in California's Mojave Desert, a sea of mirrors shimmers under the powerful noon sun. Three towers, each taller than the Statue of Liberty, rise up from the middle. Together, these structures make up a brand new electrical plant. It's the largest of its kind **fueled** by the sun. In December 2013, workers flipped the switch to power it up.

The plant uses heat from the sun to produce electricity.

The Ivanpah plant is named for the valley where it is located. It runs on concentrated solar power. The plant uses heat from the sun to produce electricity.

It produces enough energy to power 140,000 homes. Building the facility was a **challenge**. It cost about $2.2 billion and took three years. The huge plant takes up about 4,000 acres of public land. That is the equivalent of about 2,000 soccer fields.

Ivanpah came about as part of California's push to use more sunlight, wind, and other **sources** of **renewable energy**. The state has set an ambitious goal. It aims to **generate** 33 percent of its power from **renewable sources** by 2020.

❶ Sun-Powered Plant

You might be familiar with rooftop solar panels. They are used to power homes, schools, and businesses. These panels convert sunlight directly into electricity. Concentrated solar power like that at Ivanpah also relies on the sun, but in a different way.

"It takes light and focuses it into a small area to create high temperatures," says Mark Mehos. He is an engineer at the US National Renewable Energy Laboratory in Colorado. How high? About 570°C (1,060°F)! That's nearly six times hotter than the boiling point of water.

Ivanpah concentrates sunlight using 170,000 heliostats. Heliostats are huge, flat mirrors. They move with the sun as it crosses the sky. They reflect light onto the tops of the towers. The light illuminates the towers with a brilliant blaze.

The plant uses 170,000 mirrors called heliostats to reflect sunlight toward Ivanpah's towers.

The sunlight heats up water in the towers. The hot liquid boils and creates steam. The steam turns the blades of turbines to produce electricity. Traditional power plants work in almost the same way. They **generate** steam by burning fossil **fuels**, like coal and natural gas.

❷ Cleaner, Greener Energy

Right now, only 12 percent of **energy** in the United States comes from **renewable sources**. Most comes from fossil **fuels**. Why would states like California want to cut down their use? One reason: "Fossil

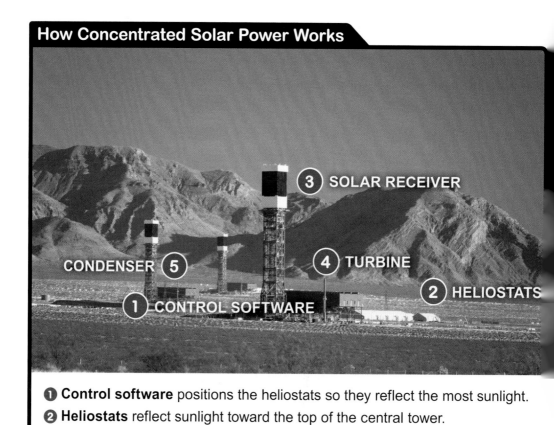

How Concentrated Solar Power Works

3 SOLAR RECEIVER

CONDENSER 5

4 TURBINE

2 HELIOSTATS

1 CONTROL SOFTWARE

❶ **Control software** positions the heliostats so they reflect the most sunlight.
❷ **Heliostats** reflect sunlight toward the top of the central tower.
❸ The **solar receiver** heats water in a boiler on top of the tower, creating steam.
❹ The **turbine** uses the steam to create electricity.
❺ The **condenser** turns the steam back into water.

forever," says Mehos. Unlike **energy** from the sun, fossil **fuels** take millions of years to form. People are using them a lot faster than they could ever be replenished.

> ## "It takes light and focuses it into a small area to create high temperatures."

Burning fossil **fuels** also produces air pollution and greenhouse gases, like carbon dioxide. These gases trap heat in Earth's atmosphere. Carbon dioxide is one of the main contributors to climate change. Aside from China, the United States produces more carbon dioxide than any other country on the planet. It produces about 7 million tons a year.

That's the main reason for California's move to replace fossil **fuels** with **renewables**, says Eileen Allen. Allen is from the California Energy Commission. "We're trying to do what we can to reduce climate change trends," she says. Solar power doesn't produce greenhouse gases. In fact, Ivanpah will reduce carbon emissions by an amount equal to taking 70,000 gas-guzzling cars off the road.

Saving for a Rainy Day

Concentrated solar power is only one part of California's plan. The state says it can meet most of its goal of 33 percent **renewables** by 2020. To do so, it will use wind power and other solar installations. But these technologies have one serious limitation. They work only when the wind is blowing or the sun is out. A coal burning power plant, on the other hand, can run around the clock.

One solution is to store power in batteries for use on overcast days, or in the evening. "But that's not on overcast days, or in the evening. "But that's not available yet on a large, cost-effective, and efficient scale," says Mehos.

That's where concentrated solar power can help. The heat it **generates** can be transferred to a huge tank of molten salt. "It's like a big thermos," says Mehos. The salt can stay hot for weeks and be used to produce steam as needed. Ivanpah doesn't have this type of storage. Newer plants will.

Costs and Benefits

Concentrated solar power has many advantages. It has drawbacks too. For one, the plants can be built only in areas that get plenty of sunlight year round. In the United States, that pretty much restricts them to the Southwest. They're also expensive, says Mehos. This is why his lab is researching ways to lower their costs.

Another **challenge** is space. Concentrated solar power requires a huge amount of land to **generate** enough **energy**. When Ivanpah was under construction, people were concerned. They worried that the massive plant would take away from the desert's natural beauty. Ivanpah's large footprint has also disturbed animal habitats. "Many of the desert's animals have been **affected** by building such a large industrial facility," says Allen. It's caused problems for one creature in particular, the desert tortoise.

The Ivanpah plant is in southeastern California, close to the California-Nevada border.

Since Ivanpah is so new, scientists are still learning about its environmental **impact**. Wind turbines went through similar growing pains when it was discovered that their rotating blades could injure birds and bats. But considering the problems associated with fossil **fuels**, many scientists believe that solar plants do more good than harm.

Mehos, for one, thinks Ivanpah is a step in the right direction. He sees **renewables** such as solar power becoming a big part of America's **energy** future. "We want to lessen the **impacts** of pollution and climate change," he says, "and leave kids a world where **energy** is sustainable."

Tortoise Rescue

Ivanpah's construction has spelled trouble for one small creature, the desert tortoise. The tortoise grows to about a foot long. Building the power plant uprooted 144 of the threatened animals from their burrows. That's where they shelter to escape the desert heat.

To help the now homeless animals, the company that built Ivanpah paid $56 million to relocate adult tortoises. They helped build them new underground homes. Young tortoises were taken to a facility. There, they'll be raised in captivity for five years to boost their chances of survival and then released.

The desert tortoise is the state reptile of both California and Nevada.

TAKE A STAND

Should humans be allowed to relocate wild animals?

Debate

What does it mean to belong?

JEFFERSON
ELEMENTARY SCHOOL
5TH GRADE
FRESNO, CALIFORNIA
MARCH 1963   10

What does it mean to belong? Everyone belongs somewhere. We are connected to places: our homes, our schools, and our towns and cities. The places we visit become a part of us, and we become part of them. We are connected to people too: our friends, our families, and our classmates. Discovering where and how we belong can be surprising.

How does it feel to be part of these communities? How do we choose where and what we belong to?

Telling True Stories

by Jonathan Blum from *Scholastic Action*

CHARACTERS

NARRATORS 1, **2**, and **3**

MISS SUE, Gary's first-grade teacher

STUDENTS

GARY

MOTHER

MISS MARINO, Gary's fourth-grade teacher

FRANKIE, Gary's classmate

GRANDMA

TULLY, Gary's coworker

PHILIP LEVINE, Gary's college professor

FRIEND

ALEX, a student

Characters are listed in order of appearance.

---

❶ INTRODUCTION

NARRATOR 1: Gary Soto is the author of many books for young adults, including *Baseball in April* and *Living Up the Street*. In total, his books have sold more than a million copies.

NARRATOR 2: Gary grew up in a Mexican American family, in Fresno, California. His mother ran their home and worked factory and farm labor jobs. His father and grandparents worked in a raisin packing plant.

SCENE 1

NARRATOR 3: Our story begins when Gary is five. His father is injured at the plant. Two days later he dies.

NARRATOR 1: As the months pass, Gary becomes angry and frightened because death took his father so young. Gary wonders if his own life will be hard and short.

NARRATOR 2: In first grade, Gary misbehaves. His teacher, Miss Sue, punishes him in front of the class.

MISS SUE: Who thinks Gary should go to the principal's office?

STUDENTS: We do! We do!

NARRATOR 3: Gary runs to the office screaming.

GARY: Nobody likes me!

NARRATOR 1: At home, Gary's mother spanks him and warns him to behave well in school.

MOTHER: I don't want you going to prison when you grow up, like a lot of the other boys in this neighborhood.

GARY: I'll be good, I promise.

SCENE 2

NARRATOR 2: Gary does not become a good student. Instead, he begins getting into fights. His mother hears about them.

MOTHER: You're a short-tail devil in need of God's blessing.

NARRATOR 1: In fourth grade, Gary's teacher makes him sit with the children who do badly.

MISS MARINO: Soto, sit in the second row with the "stupids." And pay attention to the good students in the first row. Then maybe you'll become more intelligent.

NARRATOR 2: Gary tries to find something he's good at. He's a bad student, and not very good at sports. The one thing he is good at is getting into trouble.

NARRATOR 3: In fifth grade, a boy named Frankie bullies Gary.

FRANKIE: Come here, *ese* [ESS-ay]. Give me some money.

NARRATOR 1: Gary and Frankie fight. Gary gets a bloody nose. This happens again and again.

NARRATOR 2: At home, Gary talks about his **future** with his mother and grandmother.

GRANDMA: So what are you going to be someday, Gary?

GARY: A priest. Or a hobo.

GRANDMA: Be serious, Gary. You should become a barber. They make good money and listen to the radio all day. Honey, they don't work *como burros* [koh-moh BOO-ros].

MOTHER: Grandma's right. If you don't get on track in school, you'll end up in the fields, and then you'll see how it is.

NARRATOR 3: Soon, it's the August before junior high begins. There's no money for school clothes. To help buy them, Gary goes to work with his mother picking grapes.

NARRATOR 1: His mother shows him how to bend down and cut the bunches. She has done field work since she was a child in Texas and Michigan.

MOTHER: Cut the stem all the way. Don't lose your knife.

SCENE 3

NARRATOR 2: Gary continues working in the fields during his summer breaks. He also continues to hate school.

NARRATOR 3: In high school, he finds a subject he likes: history. He also stops fighting so much. He finds a new way to get out his aggression, by joining the wrestling team.

NARRATOR 1: Gary works hard and makes it to the city championship. Gary's family comes to cheer at his match.

MOTHER: Come on, *mi hijo* [mee EE-ho]. Kill him!

NARRATOR 2: Gary loses. But everyone is proud of his **effort**.

❷ SCENE 4

NARRATOR 3: At 16, to earn money during the school year, Gary begins chopping cotton with his brother Rick.

NARRATOR 1: Gary knows that some white people in Fresno call chopping cotton "playing Mexican golf." As Gary works, he sometimes feels ashamed of being Mexican American and poor.

NARRATOR 2: The summer after 11th grade, Gary gets an even harder job, in a tire factory. A man with one ear, Tully, teaches him how to buff the tires while wearing a face mask.

TULLY: Watch that you don't catch your fingers in the tires. You could hurt yourself badly.

NARRATOR 3: Gary doesn't like the work. He explains why to his mom.

GARY: I heave and buff tires eight hours a day. I wake up feeling greasy and tired. Most of us at that factory can hardly carry ourselves with dignity.

SCENE 5

NARRATOR 1: After high school, Gary enrolls in Fresno City College. He talks to a classmate.

GARY: I'm majoring in geography. I figure I will just look at some maps, study some rivers, take multiple-choice tests, and that will be that. I don't want to write anything.

NARRATOR 2: However, after a couple of semesters, Gary signs up for a creative writing class just to see what it's like.

NARRATOR 3: Gary writes poems about his family, his neighborhood, and the farming areas he knows. His teacher recognizes that Gary has talent.

PHILIP LEVINE: Gary, you should go to a special place for writers.

NARRATOR 1: Gary goes to Wisconsin to study writing. He is 19 years old, and he has finally found something he loves to do. One night, back in California, he reads a poem to his friends.

GARY:

"After a day in the grape fields near Rolinda

A fine silt, washed by sweat,

Has settled into the lines

On my wrists and palms.

Already I am becoming the valley,

A soil that sprouts nothing.

For any of us."

FRIEND: It's true that when you get dirty in the field, it's like you become part of the field. No one writes poems about this kind of life like you do.

Gary spent several summers working in grape fields, like the workers pictured here.

NARRATOR 2: Gary's first book, *The Elements of San Joaquin* [wa-KEEN], gets enthusiastic reviews. Gary calls his mom.

GARY: Mom, I guess I won't be a barber after all. People really like my poems. I might even get to be a professor.

MOTHER: Gary, we never thought this would be your **future**. I'm so proud of you.

SCENE 6

NARRATOR 3: In 1985, Gary publishes *Living Up the Street*, a book of true stories about his childhood. The book is a big success with teens. He begins getting boxes of fan mail.

ALEX: "Dear Mr. Soto, I really love your book. It shows the happy and the sad parts of life, the ups and downs. You really describe things that any teenager can relate to. Please, please, please write back! I know you're famous, so it doesn't have to be right away."

NARRATOR 1: Gary writes more books for youths. After his book of short stories *Baseball in April* becomes a big hit in 1990, Gary visits a middle school near his home. The students make a big sign. It says: WELCOME, GARY SOTO!

NARRATOR 2: Gary speaks to the class.

GARY: I want to say, especially to the Mexican American students, that your ideas can have an effect in this **society**. I didn't feel like I **fit in** as a kid. I thought my ideas didn't matter. Now, when I see how much you like my books, I know that I have made a **difference**.

NARRATOR 3: Gary Soto is proud of being from Fresno and proud of his **heritage**. Gary hopes his success will encourage Hispanic young people to become writers.

Identity Theft

by Gary Soto

The day after Valentine's Day Ana Hernandez arrived at school early intending to sort through her batch of cards. They read BE MINE, YOU'RE THE MOST, SWEETIE, CUTIE-PIE. If only they were true. No one had ever said, "Be mine" or called her "cutie-pie," an expression from her grandmother's **generation**. These days, the bolder sixth-grade boys would scream, "You like me, huh?" Still, Ana felt popular as she sorted through her cards, her mouth sweetened by the cinnamon candy a boy had dropped into one of the envelopes. She suspected it was from Peter, but she couldn't be sure.

She was still reading her valentines when her teacher entered the classroom with a new girl. The teacher's smile made Ana curious—was it possible that Ms. Welty had received a valentine's card from another teacher? There were rumors that she and Mr. Saks, the third-grade teacher, liked each other.

> She didn't like it: someone else with *her* name.

"Ana," Ms. Welty called. "Ana, I want you to meet . . ." The teacher stalled, then smiled, a little color flushing her cheeks. "I want you to meet Ana Hernandez."

Confused, Ana put down a large valentine.

"What I mean," Ms. Welty started to explain, "is that *this* is Ana Hernandez. You two have the same name!"

The **original** Ana Hernandez glared at the **imitation** Ana Hernandez. She didn't like it: someone else with *her* name. Also, she had to admit that the *other* Ana Hernandez was pretty, an inch or two taller, and nicely dressed. And was that a cell phone tucked in the pocket of her Tommy Hilfiger jeans? And were those *real* Steve Madden shoes?

But the **original** Ana quickly replaced the glare in her eyes with something like indifference.

"You got so many valentines," the new Ana sang. She picked one up and sniffed it, her pretty little nose wrinkling in a cute way.

Dang, even her voice is nicer than mine, the **original** Ana thought spitefully. "These are some of them," she explained. "Most of them I had to carry home in a sack yesterday." She wished she could bite her tongue off and let it crawl away like a snake. That was such an obvious lie!

The new Ana smiled, and the **original** Ana wondered, *Is she laughing at me?*

It was a weird experience, like looking at a twin sister you had never seen before. The **original** Ana Hernandez pondered her ill will toward this new girl, and felt that she was being unfair. *She can't help it,* Ana figured, *that she has my name.*

The new Ana **fit** right into school life. She volunteered to be a crossing guard and helped raise the flag. She helped at a fund-raising car wash and was rumored to have played her flute at an assisted living complex across the street from school. Within a week she was chosen to say the Pledge of Allegiance on the intercom, a special honor usually assigned to students with good grades. She recited it so well that she was assigned to read the school bulletin, which always started with the menu for the day.

The **original** Ana steamed. She had recited the Pledge of Allegiance on the intercom before, but she had never been asked to read the bulletin. Boldly she approached the principal in the hallway outside the office.

"Mr. Ortiz," she asked, "when can I read the bulletin?"

"But you just did," he countered in surprise.

They soon discovered the error. The reader was supposed to have been the **original** Ana, not the new Ana. The secretary, they guessed, had made a mistake. When Mr. Ortiz offered the **original** Ana the chance to read the school bulletin, she grabbed the opportunity. But she felt slighted, and the bulletin she read to the entire school was unimportant. She reported two missing basketballs and a restroom that was going to be closed for the week.

Original Ana observed that new Ana received lots of attention. Ms. Welty would call,

"Okay, who can remember when President Lincoln—" and before the teacher could finish her sentence, new Ana would fling her arm up, bracelets jangling. The new Ana didn't do this *all* the time, only at moments when the **original** Ana knew the answers.

One day when soccer teams were chosen during recess, Becky Ramirez, the star athlete of the school, said, "I'll take Ana Hernandez." The **original** Ana stepped forward, and Becky snapped, "No, not you—the other Ana. The new girl!" That day Ana was chosen last, and on the field the ball was never passed to her.

In a classroom spelling bee the **original** Ana had to sit down almost immediately, after she stumbled on *rhinoceros*. The spelling bee became hotly contested between the new Ana and Peter, the boy the **original** Ana had hoped sent her a special valentine.

"Spell *triangular*," Ms. Welty called to Peter.

He spelled it, wincing as he struggled to get the letters in the proper order. He clenched his fists in victory when Ms. Welty said, "That's correct." In turn, the new Ana eased through the word *magnetic*.

The battle lasted 10 minutes. The boys rooted for Peter, and the girls screamed their heads off for the new Ana. In the end Peter prevailed, but the new Ana clapped for the victor and even held up his hand like a champ.

This made the **original** Ana mad. *She, the newcomer, a fraud, a mere **imitation**—how dare she touch the hand that put the cinnamon candy in my valentine card!* Ana fumed.

Ana confided in her mother while they were in the kitchen peeling potatoes at the sink. Two onions that would bring tears to their eyes sat on the counter. The daughter was ready for tears, even if they were forced to her eyes by big bloated onions.

"There's nothing wrong," her mother argued softly. Her lined brow expressed her concern for her daughter. "When I was at school, there was another Beatriz Mendoza."

Mendoza was her mother's maiden name, and Beatriz her childhood name. Now she was known as Betty, though some of her friends called her Lu-Lu. Why, Ana could never figure out, but it was a name that her mother responded to.

The **original** Ana considered being called "Annie." She then thought about using her middle name, Maria. But there were two Marias in the other sixth-grade class, and a third, Ana felt, would be one too many. She then decided, "I'll change my name," and considered Michelle, a pretty name, one that sounded French.

"Michelle Hernandez," she said to her mirror. "My name is Michelle." She giggled and then remembered that her grandmother had a Chihuahua named Michelle, a frighteningly ugly dog with bulging eyes and crooked teeth.

In class Ms. Welty would call, "Ana," and both girls would answer yes. Most times Ms. Welty was seeking out the new Ana.

> Becky snapped, "No, not you—the other Ana. The new girl!"

Then the **original** Ana concluded, "I shouldn't be stuck-up. I should be friends with her." But by the time the **original** Ana decided to warm up to the new Ana, she discovered that the newcomer was so popular that they couldn't hang. She just couldn't manage to establish a friendship with the new Ana, even when the **original** Ana confided, "You know, I have a birthmark on my thigh."

Then a new fad—jangling bracelets first worn by the new Ana—spread throughout the school. "I don't want to wear them," the **original** Ana fumed, but in the end she, too, wore bracelets and was not above jangling them for no reason except to show she was one of the crowd.

As spring advanced, bringing flowers and freshness to the air, the **original** Ana drifted away from her classmates. She spent time alone, eating her sandwich, potato chips, and cookies by herself. She began to revel in this quiet time, though occasionally she would look up and see the new Ana at the center of activity. There she was playing four-square or soccer, and escorting guests around school. She was responsible for starting a school garden—tomato and eggplant seeds were first planted in egg cartons. After they'd sprouted, mothers and fathers came to dig up the soil on a Saturday morning. That day the **original** Ana saw a television crew approaching the new girl.

"Now she's going to be on TV," the **original** Ana cried. She was. The new Ana was given 10 seconds on camera. She posed with Peter near the garden, displaying an egg carton of tomato plants.

And what could the **original** Ana do but watch the new Ana play her flute during a talent show? She had to swallow her jealousy—yes, that was it—when Peter joined her to sing a song in French!

The **original** Ana felt like the Invisible Girl. She would walk around school, and no one seemed to see her. One day in the girls' room, she looked at the mirror over the sink, and her reflection was not there.

The mirror was gone, its broken shards gathered up in

a dustpan and thrown away, but the symbolism was clear.

"She's stolen my **identity**," the **original** Ana lamented after reading an article in the newspaper about criminals stealing information about another person. She chewed a fingernail. Could this *really* happen to her? She was only 12, but perhaps years from now when she got her first credit card, this new Ana would steal it. Or maybe this new Ana would get in a car wreck and say *she* had been at fault. Then she swallowed from fear. She imagined having a baby that was claimed by the new Ana!

That night she hardly slept. She listened to a dog overturn the garbage can—or was it the new Ana digging through the trash, gathering information about their family? She peered outside but saw no one.

During spring break the **original** Ana learned that her family would be moving.

Her father and mother had spoken many times about a new house and often went to open houses on the weekend. Now it was really going to happen—and soon. Her father had gotten a promotion at work and they were moving to Escondido, 30 miles north of their house in Chula Vista.

"The new place has a pool," her father said.

A pool! Ana pictured herself diving into the water and fetching a dime on the

bottom. She pictured having friends over for a swim party. *I'll be the new girl!* she thought. *I can make a fresh start, and that Ana can have my stupid old school.*

"It's going to be nice," she mumbled in bed at night, and wondered about the stick-on stars on her ceiling. *They'll have to stay,* she assumed, *and the girl who lives in my bedroom will have something to look at at night.*

On the first day at her new school Ana was nervous. *Will they like me?* she wondered. She dressed in her new clothes, and pocketed a cell phone, her first, which she habitually opened and closed.

Her mother escorted her to the office, where Ana was introduced to a counselor, a woman with a face like a pretty flower and who smelled like a flower when she extended her hand. Two girls, office helpers, said hi. A boy, seated in a chair and with a bloodied elbow—he was still hugging his skateboard—managed to put a smile on his face.

It's nice here, Ana told herself as the counselor led her from the office. Ana could see that the school was clean and modern. The flower beds were flush with yellow and red flowers, and a custodian was mopping up a spill in the hallway.

"Here she is, Ms. Carroll," the counselor announced lightly.

Ana's new teacher approached. Ana liked her right away, and liked how she took her hand in hers.

"I hear you're a very good reader," Ms. Carroll encouraged.

"I guess," Ana answered simply.

Together they entered the classroom, Ms. Carroll prodding her gently. Another girl was hunkered down at her desk, holding a pair of large scissors. *What is she cutting?* Ana wondered, then surmised that she was making a collage.

Ms. Carroll said to the girl, "Ana, I want to you to meet . . ." She stalled, uncertain how to continue. Then she said it: "I want you to meet Ana Hernandez, our new student. Funny, you both have the same name."

The girl glared at Ana, and her scissors chopped at the air. That day, the **original** Ana became the new Ana. The *new* new Ana couldn't help but falsely praise, "What a nice collage." She brought her hand to her hair and the bracelets on her wrists jangled. The students entering the classroom asked, "Who's she? What's her name?"

"Me?" She turned around in a neat pirouette. "I'm Ana Hernandez."

Meet the Author

GARY SOTO

Born: April 12, 1952, in Fresno, California

Influences: Soto has a number of favorite writers, including Gabriel García Márquez and Thomas Berger.

Education: In high school, Soto often put off classwork to read Robert Frost, John Steinbeck, and Jules Verne. After high school, he followed his brother to Fresno City College, and then Fresno State College where he earned his bachelor's degree in English. Soto continued studying writing at the University of California, Irvine, where he earned a master of fine arts.

Works: Soto's work is often a combination of fiction and nonfiction. Many of his stories come from his experiences growing up as a Mexican American in California. Soto has written poetry, memoirs, novels, and short stories for both adults and children.

Awards: Gary Soto is the winner of a number of literary awards, including the Hispanic Heritage Award, the Author-Illustrator Civil Rights Award, the Levinson Award, and the California Library Association's John and Patricia Beatty Award. In addition, Fresno State College is home to the Gary Soto Literary Museum.

ACADEMIC LANGUAGE HANDBOOK

Use the academic language frames in this handbook as a reference during academic discussions.

> The **heading** states the overall type of discussion or interaction.

> Look for the **"If" statement** that most closely describes the specific type of interaction.

> Look for examples of completed frames in **speech bubbles**.

ACADEMIC LANGUAGE HANDBOOK

Facilitating Discussion
Collaborate to have a discussion in a small group.

If you want to ask a group member about a word . . .
- So _____, are you familiar with the word _____?

Speech bubble: I've never seen or heard the word "generate."

If you want to share word knowledge with the group . . .
- I've never seen or heard the word _____.
- I recognize the word _____ but need to learn how to use it.
- I can use _____ in a sentence. For example, _____.
- I know that the word _____ means _____.

Language Tip
Follow "For example, . . ." with a sentence that shows you are familiar with the word.

You could say, "I can use generate in a sentence. For example, the air conditioner generates cool air when it's hot outside."

If you want to share word knowledge with the class . . .
- We don't know what _____ means yet.
- We think _____ means _____.
- Our example is similar to _____'s group.

If you want to select a classmate to share ideas . . .
- I pick _____.
- I choose _____.
- I select _____.
- I nominate _____.

Discussing Ideas
Share ideas and discuss new information you learned.

If you want to share an idea . . .
- Something interesting I learned is that _____.
- I also learned that _____.
- One new fact I learned is that _____.
- Another interesting fact I learned is that _____.
- One piece of data that caught my attention is that _____.
- I didn't know that _____.

Speech bubble: Another interesting fact I learned is that only 30% of plastic bottles are recycled in the United States.

If you want to ask a classmate if you can share ideas with him or her . . .
- May I (share/discuss) ideas with you?

If you want to agree to share ideas with a classmate . . .
- Yes, of course.
- Yes, absolutely.
- Yes, certainly.

Language Tip
Complete each frame with an independent clause that restates a new fact you learned in your own words.

For example, "I also learned that schools with structured recess have less bullying."

Listening Actively
Show that you are an active listener.

If you want to ask your partner what ideas or example they added . . .
- What (ideas/example) did you (add/choose)?
- What (ideas/example) did you (record/select)?

If you want to share the idea you added . . .
- I (added/chose) _____.
- I (recorded/selected) _____.

> Read the **Language Tips** to help you understand challenging language and how to complete frames with correct grammar.

> Choose a **frame** to structure what you say. A **blank line** means that you need to complete the sentence. **Words in parentheses** mean you have a choice of using one of the words or phrases listed.

Requesting Assistance

Ask the teacher or a classmate for help.

If you don't understand what the speaker said . . .

- I couldn't hear you. Could you repeat that?

- I didn't hear you. Please repeat your (idea/response).

If you don't understand what the speaker meant . . .

- I don't quite understand. Could you give me an example?

- I am somewhat confused. Could you explain that again?

- I am not sure I get your point. Could you explain what you mean by _____?

Language Tip

In formal settings, avoid saying "huh?" or "I don't get it" when you don't understand. Instead, politely say, "I am somewhat confused. Could you explain that again?"

Asking for Clarification

Ask for more information.

If you have a question . . .

- I have a question about _____.
- One question I have is _____?

If you need information repeated . . .

- Will you explain _____ again?

If you need more explanation . . .

- What do you mean by _____?
- I don't quite understand your (question/suggestion).
- What exactly do you mean by _____?
- Could you explain what you mean by _____?

Will you explain the directions for this assignment again?

What exactly do you mean by "the topic sentence"?

Facilitating Discussion

Collaborate to have a discussion in a small group.

I've never seen or heard the word "generate."

If you want to ask a group member about a word . . .

- So _____, are you familiar with the word _____?

If you want to share word knowledge with the group . . .

- I've never seen or heard the word _____.
- I recognize the word _____ but need to learn how to use it.
- I can use _____ in a sentence. For example, _____.
- I know that the word _____ means _____.

If you want to share word knowledge with the class . . .

- We don't know what _____ means yet.
- We think _____ means _____.
- Our example is similar to _____'s group.

If you want to select a classmate to share ideas . . .

- I pick _____.
- I choose _____.
- I select _____.
- I nominate _____.

Language Tip

Follow "For example, . . ." with a sentence that shows you are familiar with the word.

You could say, "I can use generate in a sentence. For example, the air conditioner generates cool air when it's hot outside."

Discussing Ideas

Share ideas and discuss new information you learned.

If you want to share an idea . . .

• Something interesting I learned is that _____.

• I also learned that _____.

• One new fact I learned is that _____.

• Another interesting fact I learned is that _____.

• One piece of data that caught my attention is that _____.

• I didn't know that _____.

> Another interesting fact I learned is that only 30% of plastic bottles are recycled in the United States.

If you want to ask a classmate if you can share ideas with him or her . . .

• May I (share/discuss) ideas with you?

If you want to agree to share ideas with a classmate . . .

• Yes, of course.

• Yes, absolutely.

• Yes, certainly.

Language Tip

Complete each frame with an independent clause that restates a new fact you learned in your own words.

For example, "I also learned that schools with structured recess have less bullying."

Listening Actively

Show that you are an active listener.

If you want to ask your partner what ideas or example they added . . .

• What (ideas/example) did you (add/choose)?

• What (ideas/example) did you (record/select)?

If you want to share the idea you added . . .

• I (added/chose) _____.

• I (recorded/selected) _____.

Agreeing & Disagreeing

Politely tell others if you agree or disagree with their ideas.

Language Tip
When you "don't quite" agree with something, you might only agree with part of what was said.

If you agree with an idea . . .
- I agree with _____'s (idea/opinion).

If you disagree with an idea . . .
- I disagree with _____'s idea.
- I don't quite agree with _____'s idea.
- I don't quite agree with _____'s opinion.

Comparing Ideas

Discuss how your ideas are similar to or different from others' ideas.

> My idea is different from Jessica's. I think parents should limit their kids' screentime.

If your idea is similar . . .
- My idea is similar to _____'s.

If your idea is different . . .
- My idea is different from_____'s.

Restating Ideas

Listen carefully and repeat classmates' ideas in your own words.

If you want to restate someone else's idea . . .
- So you think that _____.
- So what you're saying is _____.
- In other words, what you mean is _____.
- So what you're suggesting is that _____.

> So what you're saying is that humans have a positive effect on wild animals when they restore their habitats.

If someone restates your idea correctly . . .
- Yes, that's (right/correct).

If someone restates your idea incorrectly . . .
- No, not (really/exactly). What I meant was _____.

Elaborating

Provide more information and details to support a claim.

If you want to give an example . . .

- For (example/instance), _____.
- One example is _____.

> **Language Tip**
>
> "Instance" is a noun that is another way of saying "example."

If you want to share a personal experience . . .

- I know this because _____.
- The reason I know this is _____.
- I have found that _____.

Reporting Ideas

Share a partner's or group's ideas during a class discussion.

If you are reporting a classmate's idea . . .

- _____'s idea was that _____.
- _____ (shared/stated) that _____.
- _____ pointed out that _____.

If you are choosing precise words . . .

- We thought of the precise word _____.
- We came up with the precise word _____.
- We selected the precise word _____.
- One (topic/high-utility) word we plan to use is _____.
- One (topic/high-utility) word we (located/identified) is _____.

> We thought of the precise word "encourage."

If you are reporting responses . . .

- We thought of _____.
- We came up with _____.
- We (chose/selected) _____.
- We (decided/agreed) upon _____.

Collaborating With Others

Discuss responses with a partner or group members.

Language Tip

When you are working with a partner or in a small group, ask others to share ideas by saying, "What are your thoughts?"

If you want to ask a partner or group member to respond . . .

- What should we write?
- What do you think (fits well/makes sense)?
- What do you think is a strong choice?

If you want to share your response with a partner or group member . . .

- We could (put/choose/select) _____.
- I think _____ (fits well/makes sense).
- I think _____ is a strong choice.

If you want to agree on an idea . . .

- That would work.
- That works well.
- Okay. Let's write _____.

Affirming Ideas

Acknowledge a classmate's idea before stating your own idea.

I hadn't thought of that.

If you want to acknowledge others' ideas . . .

- I see what you mean.
- I hadn't thought of that.
- I appreciate your story.

Negotiating With Others

Persuade others and support your opinions.

If you want to provide a counterargument . . .

- I agree with _____, but _____?
- That's a good point, but _____?

Clarifying Ideas

Ask for more information or confirm you understood what was said.

If you want to clarify others' ideas . . .

* What do you mean by _____?
* What exactly do you mean by _____?
* Could you explain what you mean by _____?
* Could you elaborate on _____?
* One question I have is _____?
* In other words, you think that _____?

Offering Feedback

Share your feedback and suggestions about a classmate's writing or speech.

If you want to give positive feedback . . .

* I liked how you (used/included) _____.
* You did a great job on _____.
* I appreciate how you (used/included) _____.
* I appreciated the specific example of _____ that you included.
* Your concrete detail(s) about _____ strengthened your response.
* Your use of the word _____ was skillful.

If you want to offer a suggestion . . .

* Your (writing/speech) will be stronger if you _____.
* You could improve your (writing/speech) if you _____.
* One suggestion I have to improve your (writing/speech) is _____.
* I think you misspelled the word _____.
* The word _____ is actually spelled _____.
* Adding _____ would make your response (clearer/stronger).

> **Language Tip**
>
> Complete the frames with a verb phrase to give positive feedback.
>
> For example, "You did a great job on including transitions to connect your ideas."

> You could improve your opinion essay if you include relevant text evidence to support your claim.

ACADEMIC LANGUAGE HANDBOOK

Predicting

Share what you think a text will be about.

If you want to share what you think a text will be about . . .

- I predict the text will focus on _____.
- I predict the author will primarily address _____.

Reacting to Text or Multimedia

Share your initial reactions, questions, or confusion about a text or multimedia.

If you want to share new ideas that you learned . . .

- Something interesting I learned is _____.
- One new fact I learned is _____.
- After reading the text, one detail that caught my attention is _____.
- I thought it was interesting that _____.

If you want to learn more about a topic . . .

- I'm curious about _____.
- I'd like to learn more about why _____.
- I'd like to explore why _____.
- The (video/audiobook/slideshow) made me interested in learning more about _____.

If you are confused . . .

- I still don't get _____.
- I still don't (understand/comprehend) _____.
- After (viewing/listening to) the multimedia, I still don't understand _____.

Language Tip

The expression "caught my attention" means "made me take notice."

The video made me interested in learning more about how my school can switch to renewable energy sources.

Summarizing

State the key ideas and details of a text.

If you want to ask what the key idea and details are . . .

- What is the key idea of this text?
- What is the author's main idea?
- What is this text (primarily/mainly) about?
- What does this text focus on?
- What are the most important details in this text?
- What are the key details in this text?
- What are the most essential details in this text?

If you want to state the key idea . . .

- The key idea of this text is _____.
- The author's main idea is _____.
- The text is primarily about _____.
- This text is mainly about _____.
- This text focuses on _____.

If you want to describe key details . . .

- (One/Another) important detail in this text is _____.
- (One/Another) key detail in this text is _____.
- (One/An additional) essential detail is _____.
- (One/An additional) significant detail is _____.
- Perhaps the most (important/significant/relevant) detail in this text is _____.

> The author's main idea is that some students prefer to have unstructured recess.

Language Tip

Choose a precise adjective that fits the detail you describe:

- An "essential" detail proves a point or supports a topic.
- A "significant" detail has an important influence or effect on the topic or issue.
- A "relevant" detail is related to your position.

WORD ANALYSIS

Vocabulary to Analyze Context

Use these terms to analyze and discuss the meaning of unfamiliar words.

analyze
verb to carefully examine something to understand it

analysis
noun a careful examination of something to understand it

context
noun the language surrounding a word or phrase that helps you understand it

prefix
noun a group of letters added to the beginning of a word to change its meaning
mis + understand = misunderstand

suffix
noun a letter or group of letters added to the end of a word that changes the part of speech
polite (adjective) + ness = politeness (noun)

root word
noun a word that is used as a base to create other words by adding a prefix or suffix, often coming from Greek or Latin
un + think + able = unthinkable

Common Prefixes & Suffixes

Learn these affixes to use as clues to the meanings of unfamiliar words.

Prefix	Meaning	Example Words
com–	together	*communicate, complicated*
dis–	not, opposite of	*discouraged, distastefully*
im–, in–	not	*inappropriate, indifference*
inter–	between	*interact, interaction*
mis–	bad, wrong	*mischief, mischievous*
non–, un–	not	*unstructured, unacceptable*
pre–	before	*preserve, prevent*
re–	again	*recycle, recover, reverse*
trans–	across	*transform, translate*

Suffix	Meaning	Example Words
–able, –ible *(adj)*	something that is possible	*unacceptable, accessible*
–ate *(verb)*	to make, cause, or act	*communicate, regulate*
–er, –or *(noun)*	someone or something who does	*communicator, generator*
–ial, –al *(adj)*	having characteristics of	*social, mechanical, original*
–ity *(noun)*	state of	*identity, ability*
–ive *(adj)*	having a particular quality	*effective*
–ment *(noun)*	the result	*environment, achievement*
–ous *(noun)*	having the qualities of	*mischievious*
–tion, –ion *(noun)*	the act or result of doing something	*preservation, communication*

Use the descriptions and transitions for the writing types in this handbook as a reference for your academic writing assignments.

Formal Summary

Academic Writing Type

A **formal summary** is a type of informative writing. It provides an overview of the topic and important details from an informational text. The writer credits the author, but writes original sentences using precise words. A summary does not include the writer's personal opinions.

A. The **topic sentence** includes the text type, title, author, and topic.

B. **Detail sentences** include the most important details from the text.

  • **Transition words or phrases** help introduce and connect ideas.

C. The **concluding sentence** restates the author's conclusion in the writer's own words.

Topic Sentence
Important Detail 1
Important Detail 2
Important Detail 3
Concluding Sentence

Transitions

Use these transitions to introduce and connect ideas in a formal summary.

• In the article, _____.

• First, _____.

• The author also _____.

• In addition, _____.

• Furthermore, _____.

Opinion Paragraph
Academic Writing Type

*An **opinion paragraph** states a claim and supports it with logical reasons and relevant evidence from the texts.*

A. The **introductory sentence** clearly states the writer's claim about the issue.

B. **Detail sentences** support the claim with reasons and evidence from the text or the writer's experience.

  • **Transition words or phrases** connect opinions, reasons, and evidence.

C. The **concluding sentence** restates the writer's claim about the issue.

Introductory Sentence
Reason 1
Evidence
Reason 2
Evidence
Concluding Sentence

Transitions
Use these transitions to connect opinions, reasons, and evidence.

• One reason _____.

• In my experience, _____.

• According to the article, _____.

• In fact, _____.

• For instance, _____.

• For these reasons, _____.

ACADEMIC WRITING HANDBOOK

Summary & Response

Academic Writing Type

*A **summary and response** provides an overview of the topic and important details from a text and then presents the writer's position on the issue.*

A. The **summary** includes a topic sentence, detail sentences, and a concluding sentence.

B. The **response** includes a transitional sentence that states the writer's claim, detail sentences that support the claim with reasons and evidence, and a concluding sentence.

Summary

Topic Sentence

Important Details

Concluding Sentence

Response

Transitional Sentence

Reasons & Evidence

Concluding Sentence

Transitions

Use these transitions to organize the details of your summary and response.

- In the article, _____.
- First, _____.
- In addition, _____.
- Furthermore, _____.

- The main reason I am (in favor of/ opposed to) _____ is _____.
- According to the text, _____.
- For this critical reason, _____.

Opinion Essay

Academic Writing Type

*An **opinion essay** states a claim and supports it with logical reasons and relevant evidence from the texts.*

A. The **introductory sentence** clearly states the writer's claim about the issue.

B. Each **supporting paragraph** includes:
- A **topic sentence** that states what the paragraph will be about.
- **Detail sentences** that support the writer's claim with logical reasons and evidence from the text or the writer's experience.
- **Transition words or phrases** connect opinions, reasons, and evidence.

c. The **concluding sentence** restates the writer's claim about the issue.

Introductory Sentence

Supporting Paragraph 1: Reason & Evidence

Supporting Paragraph 2: Reason & Evidence

Concluding Sentence

Transitions

Use these transitions to connect opinions, reasons, and evidence.

- One reason _____.
- The article states _____.
- Another key reason is _____.

- In fact, _____.
- According to the text, _____.
- For these reasons, _____.

ACADEMIC WRITING HANDBOOK

Informative Text

Academic Writing Type

*An **informative text** examines a topic and conveys ideas and information.*

A. The **introductory sentence** introduces the topic and states the main idea.

B. Each **supporting paragraph** includes:
- A **topic sentence** that states what the paragraph will be about
- **Detail sentences** that develop the topic with facts, details, or quotations
- **Transition words or phrases** that introduce and connect ideas

C. The **concluding sentence** restates the topic and main idea.

Introductory Sentence

Supporting Paragraph 1: Facts, Details, or Quotations

Supporting Paragraph 2: Facts, Details, or Quotations

Concluding Sentence

Transitions

Use these transitions to introduce and connect ideas in your informative text.

- One clear benefit _____.
- For example, _____.
- However, _____.

- One reason _____.
- In contrast, _____.
- According to the text, _____.

Narrative

Academic Writing Type

*A **narrative** tells a story. It can be either fiction or nonfiction. A personal narrative tells a story from the writer's life and tells how his or her life changed as a result.*

A. The **introduction** identifies the characters, setting, and topic.

B. **Detail sentences** tell the most important events of the story.
- **Transition words or phrases** show the order of events.
- **Descriptive language** makes the story more vivid and interesting.

C. The **conclusion** explains the importance of the story.

Introduction

Important Event 1

Important Event 2

Important Event 3

Conclusion

Transitions

Use these transitions to help move the reader through the events of your narrative.

- During _____.
- So, _____.
- After that, _____.

- At that moment, _____.
- Clearly, _____.
- As a result, _____.

ACADEMIC GLOSSARY

A glossary is a useful tool found at the back of many books. It contains information about key words in the text. Review the sample glossary entry below.

This is an **entry word**—the word you look up. It is divided into syllables. Words in bold are Words to Know and words highlighted in yellow are Words to Go.

The **pronunciation** comes after the entry word. Letters and letter combinations stand for different sounds. The stressed syllable is marked in bold letters.

The **meaning** of the word follows the part of speech.

The **part of speech** follows the pronunciation.

A **number** appears at the beginning of each meaning if more than one meaning is given for the entry word.

The **Spanish cognate** is a word that looks or sounds the same in Spanish and has a similar meaning.

The **origin** of the word tells you the meaning of the word's Greek or Latin root.

The entry word is used in an **example sentence** that is in italics.

be•ne•fit
(**ben**-uh-fit)

1. *noun* something that is helpful or good for you. *A major benefit of riding my bike to school is that I get there earlier.*
   Spanish cognate: beneficio

2. *verb* to help or be helped by someone or something. *Everyone could benefit from getting a good night's sleep and eating plenty of vegetables.*
   Spanish cognate: beneficiar
   Origin: Latin *bene*, meaning "well" + *facere* meaning "do"

a·bil·i·ty
(uh-**bil**-i-tee)
noun something that a person can do. *Superman is a fictional character who has the remarkable ability to fly.*
Origin: Latin *habilis,* meaning "able"
Spanish cognate: habilidad

ac·cu·ra·cy
(**ak**-yuh-ruh-see)
noun exactness or correctness in every detail. *When the test results didn't match, the doctor doubted their accuracy.*
Origin: Latin *accuratus,* meaning "done with care"

ac·tion
(**ac**-shuhn)
verb exciting or notable activity. *The movie about car racing was full of nonstop action.*
Origin: Latin *agere,* meaning "do, act"
Spanish cognate: acción

ad·dict
(**ad**-ikt)
noun a person who cannot give up or stop doing something. *Mr. Rios is a reading addict, and he always has a book with him.*
Origin: Latin *addict-,* meaning "assigned"
Spanish cognate: adicto(a)

ad·dic·ted
(uh-**dik**-tid)
adjective liking something a lot and not wanting to stop doing it or having it. *My brother is totally addicted to science-fiction movies.*
Spanish cognate: adicto(a)

ad·van·ces
(ad-**vans**-sez)
noun forward movements; progress. *Medical advances may someday give us a cure for cancer.*
Origin: Latin *abante,* meaning "in front"
Spanish cognate: avances

af·fect
(uh-**fekt**)
verb to cause something to change. *A good song has the power to affect many people.*
Origin: Latin *afficere,* meaning "to influence"
Spanish cognate: afectar

ag·gres·sion
(uh-**gresh**-uhn)
noun fierce behavior. *We want Sue to be on our team because she plays with aggression.*
Origin: Latin *aggredi-,* meaning "to attack"
Spanish cognate: agresión

a·vail·a·ble
(uh-**vay**-luh-buhl)
adjective able to be used, easily bought, or found. *Ramón wants to buy that new CD as soon as it becomes available.*
Origin: Latin *valere,* meaning "to be of value" + *-able*

a·void
(uh-**void**)
verb to stay away from or stop oneself from doing something. *When my best friend and I got into a fight, I did my best to avoid him at school.*

ACADEMIC GLOSSARY

ban
(**ban**)
1. *noun* a law or rule that says something is not allowed. *Because of the ban on junk food, the school cafeteria began serving more fruit and vegetables.*
2. *verb* to say that something is not allowed. *The principal wants to ban soda from the vending machines.*

be•long
(bi-**long**)
verb to fit in a place, group, or situation; to have the right qualities to be part of a group. *Whenever I play basketball with my friends, I feel that we belong on a professional team.*

be•longed
(bi-**longd**)
verb fit in as part of a group. *When his new classmates invited him to play volleyball, Sam knew he finally belonged.*

be•long•ing
(bi-**long**-ing)
noun a feeling that one fits in as part of a group. *Being part of the school band gives me a great sense of belonging.*

ben•e•fit
(**ben**-uh-fit)
1. *noun* something that is helpful or good for you. *A major benefit of riding my bike to school is that I get there earlier.*
Spanish cognate: beneficio
2. *verb* to help or be helped by something or someone. *Everyone could benefit from getting a good night's sleep.*
Spanish cognate: beneficiar
Origin: Latin *bene,* meaning "well" + *facere,* meaning "do"

chal•lenge
(**chal**-uhnj)
noun something that is difficult. *Uncle Steve is training for the challenge of running a marathon.*

cliques
(**kleeks**)
noun small groups of people who are very friendly with one another but who do not easily allow new people to join them. *The cliques at that school make it very hard for new students to make friends there.*

com•mu•ni•cate
(kuh-**myoo**-nuh-kate)
verb to share information or express one's thoughts and feelings. *Most of my friends use texting to communicate quickly and effectively.*
Origin: Latin *communis,* meaning "shared"
Spanish cognate: comunicar, comunicarse

com•mu•ni•ca•tion
(kuh-myoo-nuh-**kay**-shuhn)
noun the act of sharing information or expressing thoughts and feelings with someone. *My cell phone helps me stay in communication with my friends and my parents.*
Spanish cognate: comunicación

com•mu•ni•ca•tor
(kuh-**myoo**-nuh-kay-tur)
noun a person or device that shares information, thoughts, or feelings in some way. *The senator is a great communicator, for her speeches are always memorable.*
Spanish cognate: comunicador

con•cen•trat•ed
(**kon**-suhn-tra-tid)
adjective focused on a single area.
*With the concentrated force of four
horses pulling on one sled, the workers
were able to move a huge stone block.*
Origin: Latin *con-,* meaning "together" +
centrum, meaning "center"
Spanish cognate: concentrado(a)

con•cern
(kuhn-**surn**)
noun a feeling or cause of worry
about something important. *At
the city council meeting, several
people expressed concern about
plans for the new freeway.*
Origin: Latin *concernere,* meaning "be
relevant to"

con•tam•i•nants
(kuhn-**tam**-uh-nahnts)
noun substances that make
something dirty or unfit for use.
*Certain bacteria are contaminants
that can cause food poisoning.*
Origin: Latin *contaminat-,* meaning
"made impure"
Spanish cognate: contaminantes

con•ven•ience
(kuhn-**vee**-nyuhnss)
noun something useful that makes
life easier. *Having wireless service
in the home is a great convenience
because I don't have to be at
our computer to go online.*
Spanish cognate: conveniencia

con•ven•ient
(kuhn-**vee**-nyuhnt)
adjective easy to use or get to. *What
would be a convenient time for us to get
together to plan our history project?*
Origin: Latin *convenient-,* meaning
"assembling, agreeing"
Spanish cognate: conveniente

crit•i•cism
(**krit**-uh-siz-uhm)
noun remarks that say what you
think is bad about someone or
something. *The reviewer gave the
movie a bad review, but he had
good reasons for his criticism.*
Origin: Latin *criticus,* meaning "judge,
decide" + *-ism*
Spanish cognate: crítica

de•vel•op
(di-**vel**-uhp)
verb to grow bigger, stronger, or more
advanced, or to make something or
someone grow in this way. *If you keep
practicing the piano, you may develop
into a great musician.*

de•vel•oped
(di-**vel**-uhpt)
adjective larger or more
advanced. *I saw that the new
park was more developed this
week since they had planted new
trees and added a jungle gym.*

de•vel•op•ment
(di-**vel**-uhp-ment)
noun an event or series of events
showing growth and progress. *The
development of English as we speak it
today is an interesting story.*

ACADEMIC GLOSSARY

de•vice
(di-**visse**)
noun a machine or tool that does a particular job. *A pacemaker is an electronic device that helps a person keep a regular heartbeat.*
Origin: Latin *divis-,* meaning "divided"

dif•fer•ence
(**dif**-ur-uhnss)
noun an important effect or influence on someone or something. *The testimony of one witness made a huge difference in the outcome of the trial.*
Origin: Latin *different-,* meaning "carrying away"

dig•i•tal
(**dij**-uh-tuhl)
adjective involving the use of electronic or computer technology. *Digital cameras store images on a memory card, not on film.*
Origin: Latin *digitus,* meaning "finger, toe"
Spanish cognate: *digital*

dig•ni•ty
(**dig**-nuh-tee)
noun a quality that makes a person deserving of honor and respect. *The losing player acted with dignity as she shook the winning player's hand.*
Origin: Latin *dignus,* meaning "worthy"
Spanish cognate: *dignidad*

dose
(**dohss**)
noun a small amount of something. *A daily dose of brisk walking helps me keep in shape.*
Origin: Greek *dosis,* meaning "gift"
Spanish cognate: *dosis*

dusk
(**dusk**)
noun the time when day changes into night and the sky starts to get darker. *My mom calls me in from playing outside when it becomes dusk.*

ef•fect
(uh-**fekt**)
noun the way an event, action, or person changes someone or something. *The sudden rain delayed the game, but it had little effect on the crowd's enthusiasm.*
Origin: Latin *efficere,* meaning "accomplish"
Spanish cognate: *efecto*

ef•fort
(**ef**-urt)
noun the act of trying hard to achieve something. *Dad is sure that with a little more effort, he can get that old car running again.*
Origin: Latin *ex-,* meaning "out" + *fortis,* meaning "strong"
Spanish cognate: *esfuerzo*

em•pa•thy
(**em**-puh-thee)
noun the ability to understand and share someone's feelings and thoughts. *Mrs. Lee is a good person to ask for advice because she has a lot of empathy for the students.*
Origin: Greek *em-,* meaning "in" + *pathos,* meaning "feeling"
Spanish cognate: *empatía*

en•dan•gered
(en-**dayn**-jurd)
adjective likely to no longer exist very soon, usually due to human activity. *Many organizations work to keep endangered animals from disappearing forever.*

en•er•gy
(**en**-ur-jee)
noun power; often used to make heat, light, or electricity. *All of the power in that new building comes from solar energy.*
Spanish cognate: energía

en•vi•ron•ment
(en-**vye**-ruhn-muhnt)
noun the land, water, and air in which people, plants, or animals live. *In order to help the environment, I always try to pick up garbage I see on the ground.*

ex•ces•sive
(ek-**sess**-iv)
adjective too much. *I think that putting three bows on that present is an excessive amount of decoration.*
Origin: Latin *excedere,* meaning "surpass"
Spanish cognate: excesivo(a)

ex•tinct
(ek-**stingkt**)
adjective no longer found alive. *Jon would love to see living dinosaurs, but dinosaurs are extinct.*
Origin: Latin *exstinct-,* meaning "extinguished"
Spanish cognate: extinto(a)

ex•tinc•tion
(ek-**stingk**-shuhn)
noun the act or result of the death of all members of a particular living thing. *Hunting and a loss of habitat led to the total extinction of the passenger pigeon a century ago.*
Spanish cognate: extinción

fa•cil•i•ty
(fuh-**sil**-uh-tee)
noun a place or service provided for people to use or enjoy. *The library's excellent new facility includes two conference rooms, several comfortable reading areas, and a beautiful garden.*
Origin: Latin *facilis,* meaning "easy"

fil•ter
(**fil**-tur)
noun a device that cleans water, air, and other things as they pass through it. *To keep the air in the house clean, we regularly change the filter in the furnace.*
Spanish cognate: filtro

find
(**finde**)
verb to discover or learn something. *When you examine the slide through the microscope, what do you find?*

fit in
(**fit in**)
verb phrase to be accepted by other people in a group. *If you want to fit in with these jokesters, you'll need a good sense of humor.*

ACADEMIC GLOSSARY

fo•cus
(**foh**-kuhss)
verb to pay special attention to something or somebody. *Good drivers constantly focus on what is behind them as well as ahead.*
Origin: Latin *focus*, meaning "hearth"

fu•el
(**fyoo**-uhl)
noun anything that can be burned to make heat or power. *The first steam locomotives usually used coal, wood, or oil as fuel.*
Origin: Latin *focus*, meaning "hearth"

fu•ture
(**fyoo**-chur)
noun the time after the present. *In the future, will we be able to leave Earth and live on other planets?*
Origin: Latin *futurus*, meaning "grow, become"
Spanish cognate: *futuro*

gen•er•ate
(**jen**-uh-rate)
verb to make or create something. *Our Spanish club needs to generate some ideas for a fund-raising activity.*
Origin: Latin *generat-*, meaning "created"
Spanish cognate: *generar*

gen•er•a•tion
(jen-uh-**ray**-shuhn)
noun all the people who are about the same age. *My parents' generation was the first to play video games in a big way.*
Spanish cognate: *generación*

gen•er•a•tor
(**jen**-uh-ray-tur)
noun something that creates something else (often, a device that creates electricity). *When the power went out, a generator kept the lights and refrigerator running.*
Spanish cognate: *generador*

hab•i•tat
(**hab**-uh-tat)
noun the place and natural conditions in which something lives. *Building a shopping center in that place will destroy the habitat of the animals that live there.*
Origin: Latin *habitare*, meaning "possess, inhabit"
Spanish cognate: *hábitat*

her•i•tage
(**her**-uh-tij)
noun the beliefs, values, and customs that are important to a family, country, or culture. *Because of our Chinese heritage, people in my family often wear red at happy family gatherings.*
Origin: Latin *heres, hered-*, meaning "heir"

i•den•ti•ty
(eye-**den**-ti-tee)
noun a sense of self; a person's name or who a person is. *In the comics, Wonder Woman is the secret identity of Diana Prince.*
Origin: Latin *idem*, meaning "same"
Spanish cognate: *identidad*

il•lu•mi•nate
(i-**loo**-muh-nate)
verb to light something up. *At night, these new lights will illuminate the tower so brightly that you will be able to see it from miles away.*
Origin: Latin *in-*, meaning "upon" + *lumen, lumin-*, meaning "light"
Spanish cognate: iluminar

im•i•ta•tion
(im-uh-**tay**-shuhn)
noun a copy; not the real thing. *Grandma was disappointed to find out that her pearl necklace was an imitation, not a quality piece of jewelry.*
Origin: Latin *imitat-*, meaning "copied"
Spanish cognate: imitación

im•pact
(**im**-pakt)
noun the effect of one thing on another. *The decisions made by the student council have an impact on everyone at school.*
Origin: Latin *impact-*, meaning "driven in," or Latin *impingere*, meaning "drive something in or at"
Spanish cognate: impacto

in•dif•fer•ence
(in-**dif**-uhr-uhnss)
noun a lack of interest in or care about something. *Scott really wanted to hear our news, but he pretended to show indifference.*
Origin: Latin *in-*, meaning "not" + *different-*, meaning "differing, deferring"
Spanish cognate: indiferencia

la•bor
(**lay**-bur)
noun physical work. *Weeding the garden is manual labor because I use my hands to do the job.*
Origin: Latin *labor*, meaning "toil, trouble"

land•fill
(**land**-fil)
noun a place where trash is stacked and covered with dirt. *A line of garbage trucks approached the landfill, ready to dump their loads.*

lead to
(**leed too**)
verb phrase to cause something to happen or cause someone to do something. *Not getting enough sleep can lead to trouble paying attention in class.*

new•com•er
(**noo**-kuhm-ur)
noun a person who has just come to a place. *As a newcomer to this town, I could use some help in finding my way around.*

off•shore
(of-**shor**)
adjective happening in an ocean or lake, at a distance from the land. *The offshore rescue took place in the waters near Miami Beach.*

o•rig•i•nal
(uh-**rij**-uh-nuhl)
adjective first, earliest, or existing from the beginning. *The movie changed the ending of the original story so that the hero lives instead of dies.*
Origin: Latin *oriri*, meaning "to rise"
Spanish cognate: original

ACADEMIC GLOSSARY

pag•eant
(**paj**-uhnt)
noun a public parade, often very showy and majestic. *The patriotic pageant at the Fourth of July celebration featured marchers in historical costumes.*

par•tic•i•pate
(par-**tiss**-uh-pate)
verb to join with others in an activity or event. *My friends and I plan to participate in the school band this fall.*
Origin: Latin *pars, part-*, meaning "part" + *capere,* meaning "take"
Spanish cognate: participar

per•spec•tive
(pur-**spek**-tiv)
noun a particular way of looking at or thinking about something. *What's your perspective on cell phone use at school?*
Origin: Latin *per-*, meaning "through" + *specere,* meaning "to look"
Spanish cognate: perspectiva

pe•ti•tion
(puh-**tish**-uhn)
noun a letter that many people sign hoping to make their feelings or desires for change known to those in power. *We quickly signed the petition asking for a change in the school dress code.*
Origin: Latin *petit-*, meaning "aimed at, sought, laid claim to"
Spanish cognate: petición

port•a•ble
(**por**-tuh-buhl)
adjective able to be carried around or moved easily. *A portable generator made our week of camping much easier.*
Origin: Latin *portare,* meaning "carry"
Spanish cognate: portátil

prai•rie
(**prair**-ee)
noun a wide, open area of fairly flat grassland. *As the wagon train crossed the prairie, travelers saw the land stretching out for miles around them.*
Origin: Latin *pratum,* meaning "meadow"

pres•er•va•tion
(prez-ur-**vay**-shuhn)
noun the act of keeping something in its original state or in good condition. *The Historical Society is working for the preservation of this old farm so that visitors can see how people lived in the early 1800s.*
Spanish cognate: preservación

pre•serve
(pri-**zurv**)
1. *verb* to keep something in its original state or in good condition. *By framing this certificate, I can preserve it forever.*
   Spanish cognate: preservar

2. *noun* a place that is kept in its original state or in good condition. *Our class visited a nature preserve to observe the plants and animals that live there.*
Origin: Latin *prae-*, meaning "before, in advance" + *servare,* meaning "to keep"

rate

(**rayt**)

noun a degree of speed. *With medical treatment, the patient improved at a surprising rate.*

Origin: Latin *ratus,* meaning "reckoned"

re•cy•cla•ble

(ree-**sye**-kluh-buhl)

1. *adjective* able to be treated and reused in some way. *These tires are recyclable; they will be shredded and used to pave playgrounds and walkways.*

   Spanish cognate: reciclable

2. *noun* an item that is able to be treated and reused in some way. *This glass jar is a recyclable, for it can be cleaned and refilled.*

re•cy•cle

(ree-**sye**-kuhl)

verb to put used objects through a process so they can be made into something new. *Our school has special containers so that we can recycle bottles, cans, and paper.*

Origin: Latin *re-,* meaning "again" + Greek *kuklos,* meaning "circle" or "circular motion"

Spanish cognate: reciclar

re•cy•cled

(ree-**sye**-kuhld)

adjective treated and reused in some way. *I wonder what the recycled glass in these tiles was used for originally.*

Spanish cognate: reciclado(a)

re•cy•cling

(ree-**sye**-kling)

noun materials intended to be reused in some way. *We put our recycling in a bin by the curb for pickup.*

Spanish cognate: reciclaje

reg•u•late

(**reg**-yuh-late)

verb to use rules to control an activity or process. *We regulate our family expenses by sticking to a budget.*

Origin: Latin *regulat-,* meaning "directed, regulated"

Spanish cognate: regular

re•late

(ri-**late**)

verb to be connected. *The poems that we are writing in class all relate to important moments in American history.*

Origin: Latin *relat-,* meaning "brought back"

Spanish cognate: relacionar

re•new

(ri-**noo**)

verb to replace, refill, or restore naturally. *When you're tired, you may find that a short nap will renew your strength.*

Spanish cognate: renovar

re•new•a•ble

(ri-**noo**-uh-buhl)

adjective able to be replaced, refilled, or restored naturally. *You have to return that library book tomorrow; it is not renewable.*

ACADEMIC GLOSSARY

re•new•a•bles
(ri-**noo**-uh-buhlz)
noun objects or resources that can be replaced, refilled, or restored naturally. *Wind energy and solar energy are two renewables that may power many buildings in the future.*

re•plen•ished
(ri-**pleh**-nisht)
verb refilled or restored something. *The empty truck that had been salting the icy roads went back to the barn and replenished its supply of salt.*
Origin: Latin *re-,* meaning "again" + *plenir,* meaning "fill"

re•quire
(ri-**kwire**)
verb to expect someone to do something because of laws or rules. *All of the school coaches require team members to have a healthful diet.*
Origin: Latin *re-* (expressing intensive force) + *quaerere,* meaning "seek"
Spanish cognate: requerir

re•verse
(ri-**vurss**)
verb to make something the opposite of what it was before. *Everyone waited to see if the referees would reverse their decision and give our team a penalty kick.*
Origin: Latin *re-,* meaning "back" + *vertere,* meaning "to turn"

re•viv•ing
(ri-**vive**-ing)
verb bringing something back to life, awareness, or usefulness. *The school nurse started reviving the student who had fainted.*
Origin: Latin *re-,* meaning "back" + *vivere,* meaning "live"

roam
(rohm)
verb to wander around with no clear purpose or direction. *Aunt Mae loves to roam through her garden, admiring her flowers.*

so•cial
(**soh**-shuhl)
adjective having to do with people being together and getting along. *Marissa's ability to make people feel welcome is her best social skill.*
Origin: Latin *socius,* meaning "friend"
Spanish cognate: social

so•ci•e•ty
(suh-**sye**-uh-tee)
noun people in general or people as a group. *We have been learning about the different classes in ancient Aztec society.*
Spanish cognate: sociedad

sod
(**sod**)
noun the top layer of soil and the grass growing from it. *Many settlers of the west had few building supplies, so they cut bricks of sod and used them to build houses.*

source
(**sorss**)
noun where something starts or comes from. *Worn-out brake pads were the source of the squealing noise in the car.*
Origin: Latin *surgere,* meaning "rise"

spe•cies
(**spee**-sheez)
noun a group of plants or animals whose members are similar and can mate and have offspring. *The walking catfish is a nonnative species that has spread in parts of the Everglades.*
Origin: Latin *specere,* meaning "to look"
Spanish cognate: especie

stan•dards
(**stan**-durds)
noun rules or models that measure how good something is. *The coach set high standards for his players, including getting good grades.*
Spanish cognate: estándares

struc•tured
(**struhk**-churd)
adjective carefully planned or arranged. *The mayor's structured speech was designed to please as many voters as possible.*
Origin: Latin *struere,* meaning "to build"
Spanish cognate: estructurado(a)

sur•vive
(sur-**vive**)
verb to continue to live or exist. *The people who survive the hurricane will have to clean up a lot of damage.*
Origin: Latin *super-,* meaning "in addition" + *vivere,* meaning "to live"
Spanish cognate: sobrevivir

trans•form
(transs-**form**)
verb to completely change something or someone, especially in a good way. *This snowfall will transform the neighborhood into a winter wonderland.*
Origin: Latin *trans-,* meaning "across" + *formare,* meaning "to form"
Spanish cognate: transformar

un•re•li•a•ble
(uhn-ri-**lye**-uh-buhl)
adjective not able to be trusted or depended upon. *City leaders did not hire that company for the job because they had found its workers to be unreliable in the past.*
Origin: Old English *un-,* meaning "not" + Latin *re-,* meaning "once again" + *ligare,* meaning "bind" + *-abilis,* meaning "able to"

un•struc•tured
(uhn-**struhk**-churd)
adjective done with little or no planning or organization. *When I'm at home on the weekend, my schedule is largely unstructured so I can do what I want.*
Origin: Old English *un-,* meaning "not" + Latin *struere,* meaning "to build"
Spanish cognate: sin estructura

vol•un•tar•y
(**vol**-uhn-ter-ee)
adjective done willingly, without being forced. *The class trip will be paid for through voluntary donations.*
Origin: Latin *voluntas,* meaning "will"
Spanish cognate: voluntario(a)

SOURCES

Issue 1: Screen Time

American Academy of Pediatrics. "Policy Statement: Children, Adolescents, and the Media." *Pediatrics* 132.5 (2013): 958–961. Print

Bubar, Joe. "R U 2 Plugged In?" *Scholastic News* 5/6 ed 82.21 (2014): 4–8. Print.

Gable, Lawrence. "Schools Struggle With Cell Phones on Campus." *What's Happening in California?* 13.4 (2011): 2. Print.

Richardson, Hannah, "Limit Children's Screen Time, Expert Urges." *BBC.com.* BBC, 9 Oct. 2012. Web. 25 Feb. 2015.

Rideout, Victoria J., Ulla G. Foehr, and Donald F. Roberts. "Generation M2: Media in the Lives of 8- to 18-Year-Olds." The Henry J. Kaiser Family Foundation. Jan. 2010. Web 25 Feb. 2015. <https://kaiserfamilyfoundation.files.wordpress.com/2013/04/8010.pdf>.

United States. Dept. of Health and Human Services. National Center for Health Statistics. *NCHS Data Brief*, no 157. Hyattsville: National Center for Health Statistics, 2014. Web. 3 Feb. 2015. <http://www.cdc.gov/nchs/data/databriefs/db157.pdf>.

Wallis, Claudia. "The Impacts of Media Multitasking on Children's Learning & Development." New York: The Joan Ganz Cooney Center and Stanford University, 2010. Print.

Issue 2: Recess Rules!

Chiles, Mari and Olivia Vigna. "Should Recess Be Structured?" *Scholastic News* 5/6 ed 79.4 (2010): 7. Print.

Huwaldt, Zachary and Briana Walters. "Do Kids Need Recess Every Day?" *Scholastic News* 5/6 ed 75.21 (2013): 7. Print.

Juster, F. Thomas, Hiromi Ono and Frank P. Stafford. "Changing Times of American Youth: 1981–2003." University of Michigan, Ann Arbor, 2004. Web. 25 Feb. 2015. <http://ns.umich.edu/Releases/2004/Nov04/teen_time_report.pdf>.

Kazakoff, Lois. "To Fix the Classroom, Rethink Recess." *Sfgate.com.* San Francisco *Chronicle*, 16 June 2013. Web 25 Feb. 2015.

Mathematica Policy Research. "Findings From an Experimental Evaluation of Playworks: Effects on Play, Physical Activity, and Recess." Princeton: Robert Wood Johnson Foundation. May 2013. Web. 25 Feb. 2015. <http://www.rwjf.org/content/dam/farm/reports/evaluations/2013/rwjf406043>.

Robert Wood Johnson Foundation. "First-Of-Its-Kind Gallup Poll Links Recess to Academic Achievement." Princeton: Robert Wood Johnson Foundation. 3 Feb. 2010. Web. 25 Feb. 2015.

United States. Dept. of Health and Human Services. National Center for Health Statistics. *Strategies for Supporting Recess in Elementary School.* Atlanta: National Center for Health Statistics, 2014. Web. 25 Feb. 2015. <http://www.cdc.gov/healthyyouth/npao/pdf/LWP_Recess_Brief.pdf>.

Walters, Jennifer Marino. "The Power of Play." *Super Science* 21.8 May 2010:12–14. Print.

Issue 3: Extinct . . . Or Not?

"Endangered Species Act." *National Wildlife Federation*. National Wildlife Federation, n.d. Web. 23 Feb. 2015. <http://www.nwf.org/Wildlife/Wildlife-Conservation/Endangered-Species-Act.aspx>.

Gable, Lawrence. "Australia's Koalas Need Help." *What's Happening in the World?* 13.1 (2012): 1. Print.

"Living Planet Report 2014." *World Wildlife*. World Wildlife Fund, 30 Sept. 2014. Web. 23 Feb. 2015. <http://www.worldwildlife.org/publications/living-planet-report-2014>.

Sandburg, Carl. "Buffalo Dusk." *Poetry Foundation*. Poetry Foundation, n.d. Web. 23 Feb. 2015. Digital file. <http://www.poetryfoundation.org/poem/238488>.

Sandburg, Carl. "Buffalo Dusk." *Smoke and Steel*. New York: Harcourt, Brace and Company, 1921. 235. Print.

"Summary of Listed Species Listed Populations and Recovery Plans." *Environmental Conservation Online System*. U.S. Fish & Wildlife Service, 23 Feb. 2015. Web. 23 Feb. 2015. <http://ecos.fws.gov/tess_public/pub/Boxscore.do>.

Walsh, Bryan. "They're Back!" *TIME for Kids*. Time, 3 May 2013. Web. 23 Feb. 2015. <http://www.timeforkids.com/news/article-theyre-back/98981>.

"WWF Living Planet Report: Human Impact." *WWF Global*. World Wildlife Fund, 2013. Web. 23 Feb. 2015. <http://wwf.panda.org/about_our_earth/all_publications/living_planet_report/2013_infographic/>.

Issue 4: Bottled Water

2003 Market Report Findings. Rep. International Bottled Water Association, 25 Feb. 2015. Web. <http://www.bottledwater.org/economics/industry-statistics>.

2007 Market Report Findings. Rep. International Bottled Water Association, 25 Feb. 2015. Web. <http://www.bottledwater.org/economics/industry-statistics>.

2012 United States National Post-Consumer Plastics Bottle Recycling Report. Rep. American Chemistry Council and Association of Postconsumer Plastic Recyclers, 2013. Web. <http://plastics.americanchemistry.com/Education-Resources/Publications/2012-National-Post-Consumer-Plastics-Bottle-Recycling-Report.pdf>.

Brunelle, Lynn. "Think About What You Drink." *Current Health Kids*. Mar. 2011: 10–12. Print.

Fox, Catherine Clark. "Water Bottle Pollution." *National Geographic Kids*. National Geographic, 8 Apr. 2011. Web. <http://kids.nationalgeographic.com/kids/stories/spacescience/water-bottle-pollution/>.

"Is Bottled Water Really Better?" *Storyworks* Feb.-Mar. 2011: 28–29. Print.

"Ocean Confetti!" YouTube. MinuteEarth, 10 May 2014. Web. <https://www.youtube.com/watch?v=qVoFeELi_vQ>.

"Plastics, Common Wastes & Materials." EPA. Environmental Protection Agency. Web. 11 Feb. 2015.

SOURCES

Issue 4: Bottled Water (continued)

Rodwan, John G., Jr. "Bottled Water Industry: Gathering Strength." *Bottled Water Reporter* June-July 2013: 15. Bottled Water Reporter. International Bottled Water Association. Web. <http://issuu.com/ibwa/docs/bwa_jun-jul_061213b_final>.

Issue 5: Power Up

Anonymous. "Mighty Wind." *Scholastic News* 5/6 ed 79.7 (200): 2. Print.

Bernstein, Larry. "Solar on a Grand Scale: Big Power Plants Coming Online in the West." *Washingtonpost.com. The Washington Post*, 16 Jan. 2014. Web. 25 Feb. 2015.

Crane, Cody. "Bright Future." *Science World* 70.11 Apr. 2014: 8–11. Print.

Ecofys. "Updated information on the world's greenhouse gas emissions." Netherlands: Ecofys. 28 May 2013. Web. 25 Feb. 2015. <http://www.ecofys.com/en/news/updated-information-on-the-worlds-greenhouse-gas-emissions/>.

Gable, Lawrence. "San Onofre's Days Are Numbered." *What's Happening in California?* 15.2 (2013): 2. Print.

United States. Dept. of Energy. Energy Information Administration. *Total Energy*. Washington: U.S. Energy Information Administration, 2014. Web. 25 Feb. 2015. <http://www.eia.gov/beta/MER/?tbl=T01.02#/?f=A&start=2011&end=2012&charted=14>.

United States. Dept. of Energy. Energy Information Administration. *Wind Explained: Electricity Generation From Wind*. Washington: U.S. Energy Information Administration, 2014. Web. 25 Feb. 2015. <http://www.eia.gov/energyexplained/index.cfm?page=wind_electricity_generation>.

United States. Dept. of Energy. *Fourth Graders Power Their Classroom With Solar Energy*. Washington: U.S. Dept. of Energy, 2013. Web. 25 Feb. 2015. <http://energy.gov/articles/fourth-graders-power-their-classroom-solar-energy>.

Issue 6: I Belong

Blum, Jonathan. "Telling True Stories." *Scholastic Action* 22 Sept. 2003: 8–12. Print.

Ramirez, Robert, perf. Living Up the Street. Gary Soto. Recorded Books, Inc., 1995. CD.

Soto, Gary. "Black Hair." *A Fire in My Hands*. New York: Scholastic, 1990. 9–10. Print.

Soto, Gary. "Identity Theft." *Facts of Life: Stories*. New York: Scholastic, 2008. 41–51. Print.

CREDITS

Grateful acknowledgment is made to the following sources for permission to reprint from previously published material. The publisher has made diligent efforts to trace the ownership of all copyrighted material in this volume and believes that all necessary permissions have been secured. If any errors or omissions have inadvertently been made, proper corrections will gladly be made in future editions.

ISSUE 1: SCREEN TIME

"R U 2 Plugged In?" by Joe Bubar from *Scholastic News, Edition 5/6*, April 28, 2014. Copyright © 2014 by Scholastic Inc. All rights reserved.

ISSUE 2: RECESS RULES!

"The Power of Play" by Jennifer Marino Walters from *SuperScience* magazine, May 2010. Copyright © 2010 by Scholastic Inc. All rights reserved.

"To Fix the Classroom, Rethink Recess" by Lois Kazakoff from the San Francisco Chronicle website. Copyright © 2013 by The Hearst Corp. Used by permission.

ISSUE 3: EXTINCT . . . OR NOT?

"They're Back!" by Bryan Walsh from *TIME for Kids: Edition 5–6*, May 3, 2013. Copyright © 2013 by Time Inc. Used by permission of Time Inc.

"Buffalo Dusk" from *The Complete Poems of Carl Sandburg, Revised and Expanded Edition*. Copyright © 1969, 1970 by Liliam Steichen Sandburg, Trustee. Reprinted by permission of Houghton Mifflin Harcourt Publishing Company.

ISSUE 4: BOTTLED WATER

"The Bottled Water Debate" from *Storyworks* magazine, February/March 2011. Copyright © 2011 by Scholastic Inc. All rights reserved.

"Think About What You Drink" by Lynn Brunelle from *Current Health Kids*, March 2011. Copyright © 2011 by Scholastic Inc. All rights reserved.

ISSUE 5: POWER UP

"Mighty Wind" from *Scholastic News, Edition 5/6*, November 1, 2010. Copyright © 2010 by Scholastic Inc. All rights reserved.

"Bright Future" by Cody Crane from *Science World* magazine, April 14, 2014. Copyright © 2014 by Scholastic Inc. All rights reserved.

ISSUE 6: I BELONG

"Telling True Stories" by Jonathan Blum from *Scholastic Action*, September 22, 2003. Copyright © 2003 by Scholastic Inc. All rights reserved.

"Identity Theft" from *Facts of Life: Stories* by Gary Soto. Copyright © 2008 by Gary Soto. Used by permission of Houghton Mifflin Harcourt Publishing Company. All rights reserved.

CREDITS